circle,
coven
&
grove

To Write to the Author

If you wish to contact the author or would like more information about this book, please write to the author in care of Llewellyn Worldwide and we will forward your request. Both the author and publisher appreciate hearing from you and learning of your enjoyment of this book and how it has helped you. Llewellyn Worldwide cannot guarantee that every letter written to the author can be answered, but all will be forwarded. Please write to:

Deborah Blake
℅ Llewellyn Worldwide
2143 Wooddale Drive, Dept. 0-7387-1033-4
Woodbury, Minnesota 55125-2989, U.S.A.
Please enclose a self-addressed stamped envelope for reply,
or $1.00 to cover costs. If outside of the U.S.A.,
enclose international postal reply coupon.

Many of Llewellyn's authors have websites with additional information and resources. For more information, please visit our website at www.llewellyn.com.

deborah blake

❧

circle,
coven
&
grove

❧

a year of magickal practice

First Edition
First Printing, 2007

Book design by Steffani Chambers
Cover design by Kevin R. Brown
Cover and Interior Illustrations by Jennifer Hewitson
Editing by Brett Fechheimer
Llewellyn is a registered trademark of Llewellyn Worldwide, Ltd.

Library of Congress Cataloging-in-Publication Data
Blake, Deborah, 1960–
    Circle, coven & grove : a year of magickal practice / Deborah Blake.
        p.   cm.
    Includes bibliographical references and index.
    ISBN-13: 978-0-7387-1033-4
    ISBN-10: 0-7387-1033-4
        1. Witchcraft. I. Title. II. Title: Circle, coven, and grove.

    BF1566.B534 2007
    299'.94--dc22   2006048888

All mail addressed to the author is forwarded but the publisher cannot, unless specifically instructed by the author, give out an address or phone number.

Any Internet references contained in this work are current at publication time, but the publisher cannot guarantee that a specific location will continue to be maintained. Please refer to the publisher's website for links to authors' websites and other sources.

Llewellyn Publications
A Division of Llewellyn Worldwide, Ltd.
2143 Wooddale Drive, Dept. 0-7387-1033-4
Woodbury, Minnesota 55125-2989, U.S.A.
www.llewellyn.com
Printed in the United States of America

Dedication and thanks

To Blue Moon Circle: my friends, my sisters, and my inspiration. You are the family I chose, and I thank the Goddess every day for your presence in my life. Without you, this book would never have existed, and my life would be a much poorer place.

To my family, who always accepted me no matter how far I differed from the norm. If I hadn't been born to this family, I would have chosen it anyway. *Very special thanks* to my mother, who took time away from her own writing to edit this book (even sending back three chapters in a day from the RV when my last-minute rush interrupted her vacation).

To Jennifer Kemper, my first teacher and High Priestess, who started it all by inviting me to Samhain in the park. I will never forget how I felt when I stepped into that first circle. Thank you for showing me the path, and sharing all that you had learned.

To all those with whom I have practiced the craft along the way (you know who you are!) To Caere and Katy for healing and wisdom (and my beautiful HPS dedication ritual); to Ellen for never-ending friendship, cat-sitting, snake wrangling, Scrabble, and middle-of-the-night panicked phone calls; to Terry (my little kumquat); to JC for being my "go-to" guy; to JH just because; to Ellie and all the gang at the Artisans' Guild who let me play hooky from my "real job" when I needed to finish writing—you all contributed to making this book possible.

To Elysia, my first editor, always a joy to work with. Thank the gods for that "eerily empty" desk! (Timing really is everything.) To Brett and the rest of the gang at Llewellyn for making the rest of the process so easy, pleasant, and fun.

And last but not least, many thanks to my two biggest fans: Jennifer Holling-Blake, daughter of my heart, and my grandmother Jeanette (Germambie), who always believed in me. Okay, okay—are you happy NOW? Many Bright Blessings to you all!

contents

part 3: more useful information

part 1

introduction

C ircle, Coven, Grove. There are probably as many different ways to practice magick in groups as there are groups. And as with all else in Wicca, there is no one right way—just what is right for you. Covens tend to be more formal and organized than circles and groves, but this can vary greatly from group to group. What doesn't change is the commitment and intent that all Pagans bring to the practice of magick, and the benefits that can be derived from focused and inspired magickal work.

No matter whether you are a Gardnerian, Alexandrian, Green, Celtic, or Eclectic Witch, there are two basic styles of practice: solitary and group. Many solitary practitioners practice Witchcraft entirely on their own, either by choice or because there is no group available to them. Thankfully, there are many books out there to help the solitary, on every level from beginner to advanced.

Group Witches, by inclination, prefer to share their magickal lives with others of like mind, although most of them do some Witchcraft on their own as well. If they are lucky, they can find an existing group that will welcome them in, if they don't already belong to one.

But what about new groups (the members of which may not have a clear vision of how to work in unison effectively), a group that doesn't have any one true leader (a High Priestess or a High Priest), or a group that isn't lucky enough to have any members who are comfortable writing group spells and rituals?

This book is for them, and for any other circles, groves, or covens that might find it useful to have more guidance in this area. In this book, you will find a year's worth of New Moon, Full Moon, and sabbat (holiday) rituals, along with spells, advice, and other practical stuff.

May it bring you all you need to practice more fully, more powerfully, and with both reverence and mirth. Blessed Be.

CHAPTER 1

HOW TO USE THIS BOOK

The simple answer, of course, is: "Any way you want to." This is Wicca, after all. As long as you harm none, do as ye will.

A better answer, though, might be: "Whichever way works best for you."

The book is set up so that you can start with January, and work straight through to the end of December. But what if you don't get the book until March? Do you have to wait until next January to start using it? Of course not. Like the Wheel of the Year itself, this book is set up to be used in a circular fashion, starting wherever you happen to be.

Or some people might choose to start with Samhain, which many Witches use to mark the start of the pagan year. That's fine, too. Whatever suits your needs.

What about when you've worked through the entire book, and the Wheel has rolled around to another year? Well, you could start all over and do it again. Or, if you feel more comfortable with group rituals, and you want to try your hand at writing your own, there is a section at the end of each month's chapter for you to write in changes, or new rituals that you have created for yourself. (And who knows? Maybe I'll have written *A Magickal Year II* by then. Anything is possible.)

Do you have to use the rituals exactly as they are written?

Certainly not. Feel free to make whatever changes suit your practice. For instance, I have written most of the rituals to be led by one person, be it a High Priestess or High Priest, because that is the way most of the groups I know are set up. If your group is lucky enough to have both, just distribute the speaking parts accordingly. And if your group doesn't have any one "leader," you can simply choose one person to act as High Priestess (or Priest) for that ritual, or share the parts.

Can a solitary Witch use this book?

Yes, absolutely. Even though I designed it primarily with group practice in mind, the individual Witch can use many of the rituals, too. Most of the New Moon and Full Moon rituals can be used almost exactly as written, and even the larger sabbat rituals are, with a few changes, suitable for one. Again, just do whatever works for you. That's what this book is all about—making your practice as a Witch easier, more powerful, and more fun.

Do you have to perform the rituals in the months they're set in?

Not really. In some cases, such as the April Full Moon "rebirthing" ritual, that moon is particularly well suited for such work, and it might be best to do it then. On the other hand, if your group feels a real need for rebirthing in November, and the ritual feels right for you to do at that time, by all means go ahead and use it then. It is always best to trust your instincts, and the gods are pretty flexible.

Some rituals, like prosperity work, can be done during any Full Moon (or even a New Moon, if you change your approach to "banishing poverty"), and can be done more than once if you have the need.

Use your own judgment. Like an athame or a chalice, this book is intended to be a tool. It is really up to you to decide how you want to combine its use with the rest of your practice.

Of course, the easiest way to use this book is simply to start at the beginning, and to go through it until the end. Just remember that if you are new to the Craft, or are unaccustomed to group work, it is best to read the chapters about group practice and Wicca basics, and the appendix section on ritual etiquette, before proceeding with any rituals.

Like a doctor, a Witch's first rule is: do no harm. Make sure you have a clear idea of what you're doing before you practice any magick. Magick is powerful stuff.

And then, just do it. Practice, learn, live. And enjoy!

❂ Notes

_____   _____
_____   _____
_____   _____
_____   _____
_____   _____
_____   _____
_____   _____
_____   _____
_____   _____
_____   _____
_____   _____
_____   _____
_____   _____
_____   _____
_____   _____
_____   _____
_____   _____

some wicca basics

If you are planning on working with a group, you probably are already familiar with most of the basic tenets of Wicca, and how to practice it. Still, I am including here some of the groundwork for ritual and everyday Witchcraft, for those who need it. It is a good idea for your group to sit down and discuss this chapter together to make sure that you are all starting from the same place.

What is Wicca?

Wicca is both a spiritual path and a nature-based religion. It follows the changing seasons of the year, and has its roots in ancient pagan practices. The name comes from a Latin word meaning "wise one." There is an ongoing debate about whether the Craft, as it is practiced today, is actually descended directly from the teachings of the Witches of old or if it is a modern creation based on whatever knowledge escaped the Burning Times: those years when people were routinely burned for being witches, whether or not they actually were. (Much of the pagan knowledge that would have been handed down to later generations was lost or driven into hiding during those terrible times.)

Here's my opinion, for what it's worth: I don't know, and I don't care. Either way, this path works well for those who follow it, and it honors the old gods, and that is what really matters. You can come to your own conclusions, of course.

Wicca emphasizes the importance of spiritual growth and exploring the divine within and without. It is an accepting, open faith that celebrates diversity and considers us all to be children of the same Mother. Unlike adherents of many other religions, Wiccans do not believe that those who practice Wicca are "right" and all others are "wrong." Those who practice the Craft wish only to be allowed to worship in their own way without interference by others.

We do not judge others. Nor do we seek to convert people to Wicca. We believe that those for whom it is the path will find their way to it when the time is right for them. It is important to remember this if you are starting or running a group. There is nothing wrong with inviting someone who is interested in learning more about Wicca to come to a ritual or celebration; most of us start our journey that way. As long as you feel that their interest is serious (or that their curiosity is benign—remember that we also try to educate non-Pagans to undo the harm done by years of political and religious propaganda), then by all means allow outsiders to come to any ritual that does not involve intense spiritual or magickal work. But never push your beliefs—or your group—on those who are not interested. Remember that others are entitled to worship in their own ways, too.

Who do we worship?

The most obvious difference between Wicca and most other religions is the worship of a female deity: goddess, as opposed to the patriarchal male God that many of us grew up with. For women especially, goddess worship gives us a connection that many of us never have felt with previous modes of religion. But Wicca is not a religion only for women. On the contrary, because we all contain aspects of both male and female, Wicca resonates with men and women alike.

So do Wiccans worship only the goddess, or both goddess and god? Well, like so many other aspects in the pagan belief system, that varies from Witch to Witch and from group to group. Most

Wiccans worship both the male and female aspects of divinity and follow the Wheel of the Year, a cycle that celebrates the changing forms of the gods. As with all the ways you choose to worship, this choice should be based on what feels right to you and your group. Again, make sure that you all agree on this important issue before you start to practice together.

My group, which at the time of this writing happens to be all women, worships both goddess and god. We believe in the pagan tradition that says that all things on Earth contain the essence of both male and female, and that both are equally important and equally sacred.

Although Wiccans believe that all deities are one, they can go under many names and guises. And Witches often choose to call on specific deities from the various different pantheons (Greek, Egyptian, Celtic, and so forth), picking whichever ones appeal to them the most. Again, this is for the most part an individual decision, but make sure that everyone in your group agrees, at least so far as your common practice is concerned.

In my group, we mostly just call on goddess and god, and use specific names only on occasion.

One of the most important beliefs in Wicca is that we do not see deities as completely separate from us. The divine lives in us all. Because of this, we do not need a priest or minister to intercede for us—all Wiccans are priests and priestesses, capable of talking directly to the gods. So even in groups with High Priests or High Priestesses, all the members speak to goddess and god, as they will. This is one of the great joys of Wicca.

What are the rules?

There is one main tenet, or rule, in Wicca, known as The Wiccan Rede. (Rede is an old word for law.) The Wiccan Rede is very simple, and consists of only eight words:

An it harm none, do as ye will.

This means, essentially, that you can do whatever you want, as long as it harms no one. Sounds pretty simple, doesn't it? Ha! Not so fast.

Let's explore this in a little more depth. To begin with, "no one" includes yourself. This means that if you follow the Wiccan law, you can't do anything that is harmful to yourself (including, for instance, anything that threatens your health). Just got a little more complicated, didn't it?

Does this mean that no Wiccans drink to excess, smoke, eat junk food, or watch way too much bad TV? Well, no, hardly. What it does mean is that you need to strive to be always improving yourself, and work to remove or reduce any of the things that you do that hurt you.

What about sex? Many non-Pagans think that Wicca means free sex for everybody all the time. And believe it or not, they say that like it is a bad thing . . .

True, in contrast to most of the other religions in the world, Pagans have always had a much less repressed view of sex. In fact, sex is seen as yet another way to channel the gods using our own bodies, and is therefore another form of worship. Sex, in and of itself, is not considered to be either good or bad (and certainly not a form of sin, since Pagans don't believe in sin).

Does this mean that you can have sex with anyone you want? Well, sure. As long as there is nothing involved with the act that could hurt you, your partner, or anyone else. That means safe sex, willing partners, and no cheating, lying, or misleading. And you thought it sounded so simple.

So what about things like lying and stealing? Remember, if you are hurting anyone, it is against the rules. And it gets even trickier: because Wiccans believe in the power of words and thoughts, we are told to guard our words (no gossip or saying mean things to hurt people intentionally) and our thoughts (not thinking thoughts such as "I hate her").

Impossible? Well, yes, probably. But being Wiccan means that you strive toward this ideal, and do the best you can. Be kind to others and to yourself, and you're halfway there already.

There are a few other "rules" on which all Wiccans agree. One of these is *The Law of Three*. There are different ways to phrase it but, in essence, this is the belief that everything we put out into the universe comes back to us threefold: karma, if you will, with a punch. So if you are putting out positive thoughts and actions, that is what you will get back. On the other hand, if you are putting out negative things . . . well, just watch out.

What does this mean to our practical everyday lives? Well, two things. First of all, it means that if you want health, happiness, and success in your life (and who doesn't?), you need to be careful what you're putting out there. If you walk around saying, "My life is terrible," then chances are that it probably will be.

Remember that Wiccans believe that we can actually change our own realities with our will and intent. So if you focus on the positive, you can make it happen. Believe me—I've seen it for myself.

Secondly, this means that the "Wicked Witch" is a myth. Sorry if that disappoints you, but the so-called "evil" Witch is an invention of the Christian Church (politics and power struggles have been around for almost as long as religion, alas.) Seriously, think about it. If you really believe in the threefold law, would you put a curse on someone, knowing that it would eventually come back to you three times stronger? Not likely. Wish your boyfriend's ex would get pimples, only to end up with warts yourself? Not me, thanks.

Does this mean that there are no Wiccans out there using magick to harm others? Sadly, no. Just as there are Catholics and Jews who don't live up to the ideals that their religion preaches, there are Wiccans who don't follow Wiccan laws and beliefs. But they are not what we are all about, and the threefold law pretty much guarantees that they will eventually learn from their mistakes the hard way.

In the meantime, if you realize that someone in your group is purposely trying to harm others, and you can't persuade them that they're following the wrong path, your only choice is to invite them to leave. (If you are worried about them using negative magick on you, see the protective magick basics in the appendix.) And when you practice magick, whether as an individual or as a group, remember to always ask yourself, "Does this harm anyone?" before you start.

This brings us to another important rule of Wicca: *Free will for all.*

Wiccans are firm believers in personal responsibility. You can, and should be, responsible for your own thoughts, words, and actions. You cannot, and should not, be responsible for anyone else's (parental duties aside, of course).

What does this really mean? Among other things, it means that you should never use magick that would go against the free will of another. For instance, no matter what you see in some of the less reputable spell books, you should *never, ever* cast a love spell that would force someone to love you. It doesn't matter how much you think you love them, or how sure you are that you are the perfect person for him or her. If you truly love a person, you will not force your will on him or her, even if you are sure it is "meant to be." Would you want someone to do that to you?

What it really comes down to is that you should never do a spell that affects anyone else *unless you have asked for his or her permission first.* Even such beneficial spells as those for health or prosperity should not be done for anyone else other than yourself unless you have cleared it with that person first, or know them well enough to be certain that it would be acceptable to them.

Why? Wouldn't anyone want you to do a spell to make them healthy or rich? Not necessarily. The truth is that, no matter how much they may complain about it, there are some people who really *want* to be poor, or sick. It is not up to you to judge whether or not that is a good thing; sometimes that's just the way it is. But if you do a spell to improve the health of someone who has chosen (on some level, not necessarily consciously) to be ill, then you are still going against free will.

Does that mean you can never do a spell to help someone else magically? Of course it doesn't—just be sure you ask first. Some non-Wiccans might be uncomfortable with the thought of you doing a spell for them. Others might be happy that you're willing to go to the trouble, and are glad to have any help they can get. But if you are doing spellwork, remember to ask yourself: will this spell directly affect anyone other than me, and if so, am I absolutely sure that it is okay with them if I do it?

The final "rule" that Wiccans agree on is this: *Perfect love and perfect trust.* When we join together in circle, for magickal practice and to worship the old gods, we come together in perfect love and perfect trust. Powerful things happen in circle, and we all have to be more open to each other than we might be in our normal, everyday lives. We have to be able to rely on those we are working with to keep our secrets, and to work with us for the greater good.

Does that mean that you have to actually love everyone who ever takes part in a ritual with you? Yes and no. Whether or not those people are your friends, your family, or just some folks you happened to bump into at the local Renaissance Fair, while you are in circle, you accept them for who they are, as equals and as companions in the Craft, without judgment or reservations.

For once, this turns out to be easier than it seems. Something truly magickal happens in a circle that is really working, and you can feel yourself becoming more loving and more accepting. This is one of the gifts we are given by the gods. And the more you practice, the more it stays with you once you leave the circle. It can bring about amazing changes in the way you view the world, and those you share it with. Be open to it, and see what happens!

Perfect love and perfect trust also means that you try to be loving and supportive to the people in your group, even when you are not in circle. They are your chosen family (and for many Wiccans, they become as close as, or closer than, the family they are born with), so treat them accordingly. If you have a problem with someone in the group, talk to that person about it; don't just complain to others. Like families, no group is perfect, or able to get along all the time. Just treat each other with respect, be honest and up-front about your needs and concerns, and you will do fine.

When do we celebrate?

Aside from the *Esbats* (Full Moons) and New Moons, Wiccans usually gather together eight times a year to celebrate the *sabbats*, or Wiccan holidays. While the Esbats center on the moon as a symbol of the goddess, and are often used to practice powerful magick, the sabbats are more likely to focus equally on both the goddess and the god, and are primarily times of celebration and renewal.

The sabbats follow the Wheel of the Year and the seasonal cycle of changes from birth, fertility, death, and rebirth. There are many good books that go into each holiday in detail, so I will give only a brief overview here. (Feel free to skip this section if this topic is old news to you.) Be sure to note the number of holidays that have been "adopted" in one form or another by the Christian Church, and turned into familiar, modern holidays.

The pagan year starts with *Samhain* (a Celtic word, pronounced *sow-win*), on October thirty-first. More commonly known these days as Halloween (from Hallow Evening or E'en, the Christian holiday of All Hallows' Eve), this is said to be the time of the year when the veil between the worlds is thinnest. This is the time we use to say goodbye to all those we have lost in the past year, or to speak to our ancestors.

Then comes *Yule*, or the Winter Solstice. It falls around December twenty-first (solstice and equinox dates can vary from the twentieth to the twenty-second of the month in any given year. Check a calendar for the exact date.) At Yule, we celebrate the rebirth of the god as the son of the goddess. We sing songs, bring in pine boughs or a Yule log, and celebrate the rebirth of hope. (Is any of this starting to sound familiar? Most of the traditions of Christmas came from the pagan holiday of Yule.)

On February second, we gather for *Imbolc*, which celebrates the quickening of the year. The infant god grows, while underneath us the earth stirs and begins to reawaken. (Where I live, in Upstate New York, we just have to take this on faith.) In olden times, this was often when lambs were born, signaling to those who lived off the land that they had survived another winter, and would probably live to see the spring. A time for celebration indeed. Imbolc is a fire festival, and is known today as Groundhog Day.

Next comes *Ostara*, or the *Spring Equinox*, (also known as *Eostre*, after a Saxon goddess of spring), around March twenty-first. At Ostara, the world is in perfect balance between light and darkness, and so we work magick to try to bring balance into our own lives. The god is youthful, and woos the goddess in her aspect as Maiden. We celebrate spring, and rebirth, and follow the old pagan custom of painting or dying eggs, which symbolize fertility. (As you can tell from the name, what we now know as Easter was based primarily on Eostre.)

Beltane (May Eve, or May Day) falls on May first, and we often observe it starting at sundown on the night before. Earth is blossoming, the god and goddess consummate their relationship, and we celebrate the transformation of the goddess from Maiden to Mother. Beltane is a holiday of fire and fertility. We lay flowers on the altar, leave offerings for the fairies, and tend the sacred places. It is also traditional to dance around the Maypole and jump the Beltane fires for luck—preferably with someone you love.

On June twenty-first, we gather for the *Summer Solstice*, also known as *Midsummer* or *Litha*. At this time, Earth is at its most fertile and full of life. The goddess, as Mother, is pregnant, and her consort the Sun God is at the height of his powers. Midsummer is the longest day of the year, so we have plenty of daylight to celebrate the abundance and the glory of nature. This is a traditional time for handfasting rituals. (Handfastings are pagan wedding rites.)

Lammas, or *Lughnasadh* (named for the Celtic god of light, Lugh—pronounced *Lew*), falls on August first. It is the first of three Wiccan harvest festivals and celebrates grain. Remember that early Pagans depended on their crops for survival—a good grain harvest could make the difference between a hard winter and an easy one. Even though we are no longer as obviously dependent on the land today, we celebrate these holidays to remind us of our connection with the earth, and of the source of our food before we buy it at the local grocery store. At Lammas, the Corn King is sacrificed for the good of the land and the people, and we mourn the death of the Sun God. Witches bake bread, put sheaves of grain or corn dollies on the altar, and use this time to give thanks for the planet's gifts.

After Lammas comes *Mabon*, the *Autumn Equinox*, around September twenty-first. As on the Spring Equinox, light and dark are again in perfect balance. The god sleeps in the womb of his Mother, and awaits the time of his rebirth. This is the second of the Wiccan harvest festivals, when we celebrate the fruits of our labors and the culmination of our magickal efforts in the preceding year.

That brings us back around to Samhain. The goddess, in her aspect of Crone, is old and wise. She rests from her labors, and the god waits to be reborn as the sun at Yule. This holiday signals us to prepare for the long cold time, when we too will slow down, become quieter and more introspective, and gather our energies for the challenges the next spring will bring. Samhain is the Witches' New Year, a time of sorrow, as we mourn those we have lost—and of joy, as we celebrate the year just passed and look forward to the year to come. This holiday is a favorite of many Witches, and a special time to gather together in larger groups to celebrate the very essence of who we are as Wiccans.

What tools do I need?

Really, all you need to be a Witch is your mind and your heart. Pagans often use tools and props both because they make certain tasks easier, and because they help us focus. For instance, if you always pass a sage smudge stick when you are preparing to cast the circle (as my group does), eventually the smell of sage acts as a cue and helps to put you in the right mental "space."

Sage also has the magickal qualities of purification and cleansing, so we use it to prepare the site for sacred work. Various incenses will do the same thing. Some groups use one, some the other. Some don't use either. You should decide together as a group which practices you want to follow. Remember that there are practical issues to consider too—if one member of the group is allergic to strong incense, then you might want to use sage or find incense made from essential oils. (And try not to use so much that you set off the smoke alarms when you practice indoors.)

The rituals you will find in this book are taken from ones actually performed by my group, Blue Moon Circle. As such, they are designed in the format that we usually use: sage, salt, and water used for cleansing and purification of the circle, the circle cast with an athame or hand to hand, and so forth. If you and your group want to substitute incense for sage, or use a ritual sword to cast the circle, feel free. These rituals are only guidelines, and you can do whatever you wish to make them your own.

As for tools, most Witches have some or all of the following:

- ❏ **A pentacle**. A five-pointed star within a circle, usually worn on a chain, it represents the four elements: Earth, Air, Fire, and Water—and the fifth element, which is Spirit.

- ❏ **An athame**. A ritual knife used to point or direct energy, and **never** for actual cutting. It symbolizes the male.

- ❏ **A wand**

- ❏ **Candles** (see "Ritual Basics" at the beginning of Part 2 of this book.)

- ❏ **A chalice and/or a cauldron**, both of which symbolize the female.

- ❏ **A broomstick**

- ❏ **Drums or other instruments for making rhythmic sounds**

- ❏ **A Book of Shadows**, which is a book containing a record of spells, rituals, mystical, and herbal knowledge, dreams, spell correspondences (see the appendix of this book for some useful ones to start with), and any other knowledge that you gather as you learn and grow as a Witch.

I would also add to this list one of my favorite tools—books. Lots and lots of books.

One of the principles of Wicca is that we are always growing and learning, and reading the wisdom and information gathered by those who have walked the path before us is one of the best ways I know to do this. Besides, books are fun.

Who is a Witch?

Essentially, anyone who follows the path and belief system of Wicca is a Witch. Because there are so many different ways to follow the path, there are many different types and styles of "Witch." Although we believe many of the same things, we also may disagree on just as many. So, who is right? We all are. There is no wrong way to practice the Craft, as long as you follow the few simple rules I mentioned earlier in this chapter. We are all children of the same goddess—and as long as we agree on that, we don't have to agree on everything else.

Do you have to be dedicated to the Craft by a High Priest or High Priestess in order to be a "real" Witch? There are certainly some sects of Wicca whose members believe that to be so, but I—and many other Witches—don't agree. As with all else in Wicca, intent is most important here. You can dedicate yourself to the path in any way, as long as you are serious about making the commitment.

I know of one group that, lacking a High Priestess, took turns dedicating each other. The important thing is that whatever you do works for you, and for your group, and is done with reverence for the gods and for each other.

Wiccans come in all sizes and shapes, and from all walks of life. In my group, for instance, we have had a nurse, a college professor, a shop manager, and a library professional, among others. Not exactly who most people think of when they hear the word "Witch."

The most important thing to remember is that Wicca is a way of life, as much as it is a religion. You can't just celebrate the fun holidays, and forget about it the rest of the time. Wiccans try to "walk the walk" and not just "talk the talk." Doing so means caring for each other, and for Earth our Mother. It means learning and growing, and coming together in reverence and mirth to worship the old gods, and follow the ways of our ancestors.

If this sounds like you, then you are a Witch. Welcome, and blessed be.

✺ Notes

_____   _____
_____   _____
_____   _____
_____   _____
_____   _____
_____   _____
_____   _____
_____   _____
_____   _____
_____   _____
_____   _____
_____   _____
_____   _____
_____   _____
_____   _____
_____   _____
_____   _____
_____   _____

CHAPTER 3

GROUP PRACTICE ESSENTIALS

I f you are already in an established group—be it circle, grove, or coven—you may not need much
of the information in this chapter. (Read it anyway; you never know. Besides, I'll feel better.) But if
you are in the process of starting a new group, or are just thinking about the possibility, I have a few
words of wisdom to share with you, which I hope might make the journey easier.

To begin with, I'll tell you about my journey. I practiced with a group led by a long-time High
Priestess for the first five or so years of my involvement with Wicca—it was a great experience, and I
learned a lot (including a few "not-to-dos") that eventually helped me when I started my own group.

At a certain point, though, I began to get the feeling that it was time for me to move to the next
level, and so I asked my High Priestess to help me work on my year-and-a-day High Priestess training.
For those in a traditional path (Gardnerian, or the like), this usually comes after a set time (often a year
for each degree), and in a set way. Since my group was made up of Eclectic Witches, we didn't follow
a specific degree system, or set of rules. Jennifer, my High Priestess, simply started me on the road by

suggesting books for me to read and areas in which to hone my skills. She also had me do more and more of the ritual leadership for our group, including some of the large public rituals that we put on at a local Unitarian Church at Yule, Imbolc, and other times. This practice became the foundation from which I led my own group.

After a time (slightly more than the year and a day, but when I felt ready), I dedicated myself to the goddess and the god as a High Priestess, and vowed to do my best to serve them in this new role.

Then, I waited.

What's that, you say? In fact, my High Priestess dedication was in October, right before Samhain, and I didn't start my own group until the following Spring Equinox. Why? All I can say is, it just wasn't time. The longer you practice, the more you learn to recognize that "this is right" feeling. So, while I laid the groundwork (talked to people who might be interested, thought about what kind of group I wanted) during the next five months, it wasn't until Ostara that I led my first official ritual as High Priestess in my own right.

Following that, I put my group together—and, as is often the way—it didn't end up being any of the things I had planned. What can I say? The gods work in mysterious ways.

Still, what I got was so much more than what I expected. I planned on many members; I got three (at least to start). I planned on a group comprised entirely of people I was already close to and comfortable with; I got two virtual strangers. And yet, the group was more powerful than I ever expected, and fulfilling beyond anything I had ever thought possible.

So what is the lesson here? If you feel as if it is time to start your own group, it probably is. (Make sure that you are listening to the gods here, and not just your own ego.) If you think you know how things are going to turn out . . . you probably don't. Follow your heart, and your inner wisdom, and you may just end up with more than you could have ever wanted.

• • •

Enough about me. My guess is, your journey has been different than mine. Maybe you came from a more regimented tradition (Gardnerian, Alexandrian or the like), but you still feel a little wobbly in your first venture on your own. Or maybe you're not a "word person," and you are just not good at writing your own rituals. It could be that, like many of us, your spiritual practice is very important to you, but so is the rest of your life, and you just don't have time to do it all . . .

It is my hope that this book will help you to be a group Witch and take a little of the pressure off at the same time. To that end, here are the answers to a few of the basic questions I often get about group practice:

How does a Wiccan group work?

Remember that even if everyone calls it "Raven's Group" (or whatever), the group belongs to everyone, equally. Encourage all the members in the group to participate in one way or another, at the level that they're comfortable with. This will vary from Witch to Witch, depending on experience and personality, but try to include everyone as much as possible. Have some people call quarters (even if you have to write them out ahead of time so that people don't feel too nervous). Maybe one of your members can smudge the circle with sage. If someone is too shy or uncertain to participate in ritual activities, invite them to make the cakes for cakes and ale. Be patient with those who are introverted or timid, but continue to gently encourage them to participate. This is part of being a group Witch.

How often should a group meet?

Schedule meetings according to the needs and desires of the members of your group. This will vary greatly from circle to circle. The first group I belonged to met every week on Thursday nights. We did New Moons and Full Moons if they fell on or near that night, and usually made special plans for sabbats (holidays). But everyone knew that if it was a Thursday night, we'd be at Jennifer's house. In many ways this was great, but on the downside, it was a lot of time to commit if you also had a lot of other things going on in your life.

My new group, Blue Moon Circle, on the other hand, meets every month for New Moons and Full Moons, plus whichever holidays fall in that month. It makes scheduling a bit trickier, and I need to send out postcard reminders every month with dates and events, to help people keep things straight. It is a little more work for me, and circle members have to make an effort to keep track of when we are meeting.

But we decided that we really wanted to try to have a moon-oriented practice, so for us, it is worth the juggling of everyone's schedules that this kind of practice involves. (Okay, so Full Moon is actually Monday, but someone has another commitment that night . . . can everyone manage Sunday night instead?)

•　•　•

There is no one right way. Talk to the members of your group, and figure out what works best for the greatest number of people. Try not to exclude anyone, although there are going to be some times that not everyone will be able to make it.

Remember that, while it is important to practice magick at the most powerful times and to honor the gods on the correct days, it is at least as important to include as many of your folks as possible, without making anyone too crazy.

I was taught (and it feels right to me) that it is appropriate to celebrate Moons and holidays within two days in either direction of the actual date. So, while it might be more powerful to celebrate Summer Solstice on its actual date of June twenty-first, if that date falls on a Tuesday, and no one would be able to come, it is certainly allowable to have your celebration on the Sunday before. If you put forth the right energy and intent, the gods will understand.

How do I start a new circle or coven?

How do you start a group, if there isn't one near you, or if you don't feel that you would fit into the one that is? First, look inside, and make sure that you are really ready to take this step. Being High Priestess, or High Priest, of your own group is a big commitment. People look at you differently. You will look at yourself differently. It is not something to take lightly.

On the other hand, our community needs more good leaders. So, if you really are ready, that's great. Welcome, and blessed be!

If you are hiving off from an existing group, there may be some people who feel the need for a change (or who are especially close to you), and will come with you. Or you may know some solitary Witches who are ready to try practicing with others. (Both the other women who joined my group in the beginning had been solitaries for many years, but had not found a group with whom they felt comfortable. Or maybe they just weren't ready. In any case, when we practiced together, we "fit.")

Don't just take people into your group for the sake of having enough people, or because you are flattered that they want to join you. Even if you are not making the formal commitment of a coven (which I don't suggest doing until you have practiced together for a while—usually at least a year and a day), there is an intense bond that results from being in a group together. Remember, you need to have "perfect love and perfect trust." That means you have to at least *like* the people you are in circle with, although they don't have to be your best friends.

Do pick people who want to practice the same way you do. While it may not be impossible, it would be pretty difficult to have a circle with one Gardnerian, one Alexandrian, a Druid, and a couple of Eclectics. On the other hand, Eclectic Witches may find that they have enough of the basics in common with a Green Witch and a Celtic Witch to work together comfortably. Make sure that everyone understands what kind of Witchcraft you intend to practice from the very beginning, in order to avoid unpleasant arguments later.

Be flexible. As I mentioned, I started out with a particular vision of how my circle would be, and the realities ended up being much different. But if I had insisted on sticking to my original plan, then I would have missed the wonderful circle I actually ended up with. Try to go with the flow, at least as long as doing so takes you in a positive direction.

And remember that nothing stays the same. In our first year of practice, my circle focused primarily on the practice of Witchcraft, and getting to know each other better. After that, we decided that we wanted to bring in more of the "study group" aspect of a circle—learning and sharing knowledge about Wiccan history, practices, ethics, and so forth. So, some months we might meet at New Moon, but have someone present information on the use of herbs in magick instead of having an actual ritual. Or that person might talk about herbs, but also bring a spell that uses some of the herbs she talked about, which we would all do together at the end.

The point is; we did things somewhat differently in year two than we did in year one. And that's fine. There is no growth without change.

Just make sure that everyone agrees to the changes, and is happy with them. I gave everyone a sheet with a list of topics for study and discussion, and had them tell me which ones they were the most interested in, and which ones they felt that they might have enough knowledge about to share with the rest of the circle. Then we went on from there.

Remember these two words: *reverence* and *mirth*. The main purpose of any Wiccan circle or coven is the worship of the old gods. Wicca is not a game. It is a religion, a spiritual path, and a way of life. Be respectful—of the gods, and of each other. Remember to say "thank you."

At the same time, don't forget to have fun. Remember what it says in *The Charge of the Goddess*: "All acts of love and pleasure are my rituals."

Put on your garb, light the candles, and enjoy being with those who believe as you do. Laugh, drum, chant. This is the path you have chosen to walk—walk it with joy.

• • •

What do you do if you have a number of people who want to practice together, but no one person who feels ready to be High Priest or High Priestess?

I actually know a group in this situation. These Witches have been practicing together for many years with no one "leader," although one of the women tends to do the scheduling, organizing, and so on. They take turns leading rituals and manage just fine that way. Once again, it just comes down to doing things in the way that feels right to those involved, and that suits the needs of the group.

One last note about group practice: a coven is not a support group. Yes, you are there to work together, and the special bond between circle or coven members means that you usually end up sharing with each other your joys and your sorrows. By all means, be helpful and be supportive.

But—and this is a big "but"—*do not* spend all your time and energy talking about whatever problems the people in your group are having in their lives. Whenever possible, focus on the positive and not the negative. And beware of the person who seems to *always* be in crisis, and who ends up sucking the energy from the group without ever making any positive changes in his or her life. (Sadly, there are a lot of these folks out there in the pagan community, just like everywhere else.)

You can try sitting that person down and talking to her (or him) about the need to walk the walk, and not just talk the talk (that is, you can't just do a prosperity spell; you actually have to go out and look for a job, too.) Allow time for a change to take place, but if she can't or won't change, you will face the difficult task of telling her that she is probably not quite ready for group practice, or at least that you no longer feel she is right for your group.

Be loving and nonjudgmental, but be firm. Your circle is depending on you to provide an environment where everyone can practice magick with power and purpose.

People who don't have the focus for intense group work can always be invited to join you for the less crucial holiday celebrations. My group celebrates most of these as "open" circles, and allows attendance by just about anyone: "peripheral pagans" (people who have pagan leanings, but don't actually practice), group members' significant others, folks who are interested in learning more about Wicca but who aren't sure yet if it is for them, and the assorted serious Pagans that we know and love, but who don't fit into the regular group for an assortment of reasons, including the ones above. Holidays are also a great time to get together with other area groups, if there are any.

This approach lets us enjoy the best of both worlds: an intense, focused, productive monthly practice with a small, close-knit group, and the occasional joyous celebration with a much larger and more varied bunch.

❂ Notes

_____   _____
_____   _____
_____   _____
_____   _____
_____   _____
_____   _____
_____   _____
_____   _____
_____   _____
_____   _____
_____   _____
_____   _____
_____   _____
_____   _____
_____   _____
_____   _____
_____   _____
_____   _____

part 2

a year
of rituals

A few practical notes on ritual basics

No two rituals are the same. Even if you repeat the same ritual over and over, the energy will vary with the people involved, depending on how they feel at that particular moment in time. There are, however, some basic components that go into creating and enacting most formal magickal work. (You can, of course, just walk into the woods and speak to the gods, but that's not what we're talking about here.) Once you are familiar with these elements, you can write your own rituals or use the spellwork in the following section with ease.

I have listed these components in the order in which they appear in a ritual, with a basic explanation for each one. You can choose which elements to include or to leave out—just keep in mind that there are often particular magickal reasons why they have traditionally been used in circle work.

Welcome

For the larger rituals (such as sabbats), which tend to be more formal and often involve people from outside your own group, you may wish to start with a little speech welcoming everyone and explaining what the ritual is all about. This step is already included in the sabbats in this book.

Entering the circle

You may begin with everyone already standing in the circle area, or you may "process" in (walk in slowly, one by one), and have a group member greet all the participants as they enter the circle. Some groups do this with every ritual, no matter what the occasion, since it helps people to focus and put them in the "circle mood." If you want an added element of ceremony, the greeter can anoint each participant with magickal oil as they enter the circle. (See the February Full Moon for instructions on making magickal oils.)

Cleansing and consecrating the space

One of the most important ideas to remember when practicing Witchcraft is that when you cast a circle, that circle becomes sacred space. Unlike many other religions, where a particular building—

such as a church or a temple—is set aside for spiritual use, in Wicca we create sacred space whenever and wherever we need it.

If you are lucky, your group may have a permanent place that you use for magickal work whenever you get together. Or if you take turns doing Full Moons at different members' houses, you may have to create sacred space from scratch each time you meet. In good weather, Blue Moon Circle practices in the formal nine-foot stone circle I built out behind my barn. In bad weather, we simply use my living room. Since Wicca is a nature-based religion, it is always great if you can do your magickal work outside. Realistically, doing so isn't always possible. If you can't be outside, try to bring inside some natural elements—flowers, rocks, feathers, and the like—to keep your practice in touch with that essential power.

Whether you are using an established circle, or starting one anew, you will always begin ritual work by cleansing and consecrating the area in which you intend to cast your circle. There are a number of ways to do this, and you may choose to use one or all of them, depending on the ritual.

Keep in mind that this aspect of ritual serves two purposes. First, it readies the space for safe and powerful magickal use. Second, it helps us to separate ourselves from the mundane world, and to focus on the magickal work to come. Experienced Witches may not need to do as much of this preparation as inexperienced Witches will, but it is best to include at least one of the following methods for cleansing and consecration:

- Sweep around the circle space with a broom (one kept for magickal use)
- Walk around the outside of the circle with sage or incense, OR
- Pass sage or incense around the circle (sage is a Blue Moon favorite)
- Walk around the circle sprinkling salt, water, or a combination of the two, OR
- Pass a dish with salt and water mixed together, and have circle members anoint themselves with the mixture—usually on the brow, lips, and heart
- Ring a bell, or strike a gong. If you do this at the start of rituals on a regular basis, the sound serves as a signal to your subconscious, as will the smell of sage.

There are many other ways to create the proper mood and space, but these are the ones Blue Moon Circle uses most often. For smaller rituals, we usually pass sage, then salt and water. For larger rituals, we often do them all.

Cast the circle

This is a simple, but all-important step. With this act, you state your intention to create a sacred space, apart from the everyday world. You can cast the circle formally, by having whoever is acting as High Priest or High Priestess walk around the outside of the circle with his or her athame or magickal sword pointing at the ground. Words for circle casting can be found in chapter 17 of this book, and they are also included in some of the sabbat rituals.

Or you can cast the circle "hand to hand" by simply joining hands one at a time going around the circle, starting and ending with the High Priestess. In this case, you state your intent by having the High Priestess say, "We cast the circle hand to hand" as she reaches her hand out to the Witch sitting to her left. (Always go clockwise—or deosil—in a circle, except when you are specifically doing "unbinding" work.)

Remember that once the circle is cast, no one can enter or leave without having someone else open a magickal doorway. Until the circle is opened, you are in a safe and sacred space—apart from the rest of the world, outside of time and space. Behave accordingly.

Call the quarters

Once the circle is cast, most Witches call the quarters, invoking the four elements to guard the circle against negativity and intrusion. We usually start with East (some Witches start with North), the element of Air, then move clockwise around the circle to end at North. Each quarter is usually called by a different circle member, who then lights a candle in the appropriate color. Detailed quarter calls can be found in chapter 17, for those who need more help in this area.

Invoke the god and goddess

Unlike calling the quarters, in which we summon the elements to do our bidding, when we invoke the goddess and the god, we are asking them politely if they would be willing to join us in our circle. Always ask in a tone of respect, and they will likely come. I have never taken part in a circle when I could not feel their presence, although sometimes it is stronger than others. Again, you can find more details in chapter 17, if you haven't done this before.

Main ritual

This is where you do the "work" of the ritual. Everything that came before has led up to this moment. You have created your sacred space and focused your mind, heart, and spirit. Now you are ready to craft your magick.

At this point, the High Priest or High Priestess will usually state the intent of the ritual. Someone with a soothing voice who reads well, not necessarily the High Priest or High Priestess, may lead a meditation to help everyone focus on the magickal work at hand. Sometimes the group will do a task, such as creating a magickal charm or oil.

This is usually followed by the building of a "cone of power"—a focused, intentional build-up of potent energy in the circle. This energy will then be used to give power to the spell or magickal working.

Witches generate this energy in various ways, but most commonly by drumming, chanting, and dancing. Your group members will probably find that they are most comfortable with one method, but feel free to use whatever seems to work best for the ritual you are doing.

Once the energy reaches its peak, you will release it into your spell and send it out into the universe. You will get a feeling for this after a few rituals, but don't worry about getting it wrong at first—remember that intention counts. It is important to ground yourself after releasing the energy. Most Witches simply put their hands on the ground (or floor) for a few minutes until they can feel the energy dissipate. If you skip this step, you are likely to find yourself as wired as if you had drunk three cups of coffee, and unable to sleep until long after the ritual is over.

Cakes and ale

After everyone has grounded and taken a deep breath, the High Priest and/or High Priestess will pass cakes and ale. These are symbolic, and do not have to be an actual cake or ale. In part, this component of the ritual is a celebration of the gifts of food and drink that the gods give us. On a more practical note, food helps us to ground ourselves after the intense energies of the ritual.

The cake can be as simple as a loaf of bread that everyone will tear a piece from as it comes around the circle, or as elaborate as fancifully decorated moon-shaped cookies. Often the "cake" at a sabbat will reflect the holiday you are celebrating. For instance, you can serve crackers with seeds on top or deviled eggs at Spring Equinox.

The ale can be as simple as spring water or it can be a fabulous homemade mead. Keep in mind that you will not want to serve alcoholic beverages if there are children in circle, or if alcohol is a problem for any of your circle members. Cider or pomegranate juice always make festive and appropriate substitutes for wine or ale.

Passing of the speaking stick

During this part of the ritual, a "speaking stick" is passed from person to person, and each participant has a chance to say what is in his or her heart. Every group uses something different for this—it can be an actual stick, or it can be a special feather or crystal that is used for this purpose. Just make sure that whatever you use is easy to hand from person to person. Only the individual holding the stick may speak. Everyone else should pay attention and listen respectfully. For some people, this may be the only time in their lives when they feel free to say exactly what they think or feel. Remember to listen with perfect love and perfect trust, and without judging.

It is absolutely crucial that everyone observes this important rule: what is said in circle stays in circle. Never, ever repeat anything that has been told in confidence within the circle.

Anyone who prefers not to speak can hand the stick off to the next person. There is no rule that everyone has to say something. Some groups will pass the stick around as many times as necessary, until everyone has said everything they need to say. Some groups only pass it around once. Blue Moon Circle does either, depending on time constraints.

Sometimes you get someone who talks on . . . and on. Try to be as patient as possible and, if necessary, have the High Priest or Priestess gently remind that person that others are waiting to speak.

Dismiss the quarters

This reverses your actions when calling the quarters. Starting with North—where you ended when calling—you now go counterclockwise, to West, South, and then finally East. Thank each element for its help and protection, and give it permission to leave the circle.

Thank the god and goddess

Thank the god and goddess for their presence in your circle, and for their help with your magickal work.

Open the circle

You can do this in the reverse of whatever method you used to cast the circle. For instance, if you walked around the outside of the circle with your athame to cast the circle, to dismiss you would walk around counterclockwise, or widdershins. If you cast the circle hand to hand, you can all join hands, and then let go one by one.

Blue Moon Circle often opens the circle by reciting together one of the short versions of the Wiccan Rede—found in some rituals and also in chapter 17 of this book—or simply by saying the traditional closing words: "The circle is open, but never broken. Merrie meet, merrie part, and merrie meet again."

• • •

There are some additional details and examples of ritual practices in chapter 16 and chapter 17, which your group may find helpful. Just remember to work for the good of all, and according to the free will of all, and you will do just fine.

A couple of practical notes

In some rituals, especially the larger ones, most or all of the ritual takes place with everyone standing for the entire time. Sometimes, particularly when working on crafting an oil or charm, it is much easier to be sitting. It is really up to you and your group to decide what makes you the most comfortable. However, everyone who is able to should stand during the actual circle casting, the calling and dismissal of the quarters, and the invoking and thanking of the gods.

As I said in the first section of the book, some groups have both a High Priestess and a High Priest (the traditional form), some have only one or the other, and some don't have either. In the rituals in this book, I have used the abbreviation HPS for High Priestess and HP for High Priest to denote the appropriate person to read that part of the ritual. If you have both a HPS and a HP, they can take turns reading parts. Otherwise one person can do them all. If you have neither, you can have one circle member read all the "leading" parts, or you can each do some. There is no wrong way to do this.

It is traditional to have the High Priestess invoke the goddess, and the High Priest invoke the god. If you have no men in your circle, it is fine to have the High Priestess invoke them both. If you have a HPS and no HP, but there are male members of your group, it is appropriate to have them call the god anyway.

One final note on moon practices

No two Witches agree exactly on the practice of magick at New Moon. (Let's face it—no two Witches agree exactly on much of anything . . . it's what makes us all so much fun to be around.) Some see New Moon as a time to practice only banishing magick (getting rid of things). Some see it as the beginning of the waxing moon, and therefore the perfect time to start magick for increase.

By now, if you have read the chapters at the start of this book, you can probably guess how I view this quandary: I pretty much ignore it, and do whatever feels right to me in that particular month.

If you want to get rid of something—such as stress or fear—this is the perfect time to do that kind of magickal work. On the other hand, if you want to work on bringing something into your life—such as prosperity, health, or love—you can do a spell starting on the New Moon and then repeat it every night until the Full Moon.

Follow your heart, listen to your inner voice, and if you're still not sure, ask the gods for guidance.

☻ Notes

_____   _____
_____   _____
_____   _____
_____   _____
_____   _____
_____   _____
_____   _____
_____   _____
_____   _____
_____   _____
_____   _____
_____   _____
_____   _____
_____   _____
_____   _____
_____   _____
_____   _____
_____   _____

CHAPTER 4

january

January is a quiet month. After the hustle and bustle of the busy holiday season, it is a time to slow down, take a deep breath, and enjoy a welcome break from celebration and fuss. Now is a good time for looking inward instead of outward, for small get-togethers instead of large ones.

If your circle or coven is just starting out, this is the perfect time to get to know one another better, and to start forming tighter bonds as a group. Even if you have been practicing together for a while, if you have not done a group dedication, or worked on your Books of Shadows together, this is a great point at which to do so. (If you are starting out at another time of year, but still want to do this month's activities first, feel free to switch things around.)

When Blue Moon Circle met to perform our Book of Shadows consecration and blessing, we did two other things as part of that ritual: we all brought our Books of Shadows to circle and shared them with each other, and we started a group Book of Shadows that belonged to Blue Moon Circle as a whole, rather than to any individual Witch.

These actions were both important—as well as educational, moving, fun, and a demonstration of our commitment to the group and to each other. They allowed us to learn and grow, to share our knowledge, to show our trust for one another, and to start a book that would continue to grow with the group over time.

Today, the Blue Moon Circle Book of Shadows contains not only a record of all the rituals and spells that we have performed as a group, but also pictures and mementos of our time together. Although the members of the group may change over the course of years, our Book of Shadows will remain as a tool and a treasure trove of knowledge for all those who follow. And that is what a Book of Shadows is all about.

January New Moon

Book of Shadows blessing and consecration

A Book of Shadows is the name given to the book that a Witch uses to keep track of spells, ingredients used, rituals performed, correspondences, and anything else that he or she uses in the course of his or her practice of Wicca. It can be as plain as a loose-leaf notebook, or it can be a fancy pre-made book (there are many available from Wiccan shops and websites.)

Some Witches have more than one. Some are very simple, and some are filled with colorful illustrations, contain extensive notes, and are written in special inks. Your book should suit you and your needs, and the book your group creates together should do the same. Nothing that goes into your group book should be shared with anyone outside the group without the permission of all members.

supplies:

❑ A blank Book of Shadows to use for the group, and one for any member who does not already have one. You can use crayons, paints, or colored pens to decorate the group book. It is helpful for this and other rituals to make copies for everyone of the spells you will be saying.

Note: Ritual instructions are laid out in detail in this ritual for those with little or no experience with group circle work. More abbreviated instructions will be used in the rituals that follow.

• • •

- Consecrate and cleanse the ritual space by passing a sage smudge wand or a stick of incense around the circle from one person to the next. Sage should be wafted up and down the body to clear away any negative energy.

- Cleanse those in the circle by passing around a small bowl of water mixed with sea salt. Start with the salt and water in separate containers—these can be as simple or as ornate as you like. The High Priestess (or High Priest) should pour a small amount of both into a bowl and mix with the tip of her athame or her finger; if she likes, she can say something like, "Salt into water, water into salt. Wash away all that is negative; bring in all that is positive and beneficial.

So mote it be." It is customary to dip a finger into the salt/water mixture and dab it on the third eye (between the eyebrows), the lips, and the heart. The bowl is then passed to the next person. Silence should be observed during these steps, so that all those present can focus and center themselves.

- Cast the circle. You can cast it hand to hand or by having whoever is acting as HPS or HP walk around the outside of the circle with an athame. It is okay to be sitting up until this point, but you should always stand up to call the quarters and invoke the goddess.
- Call the quarters. The following quarter calls are just examples. Feel free to use any words that come to you.

East:

I call the Watchtower of the East, the spirit of Air. Help us to keep our minds clear and open, and aid us in seeking positive change. Come now and guard our circle. Welcome, and blessed be.

Light a yellow candle in the East place on the altar, or by the East's point on the edge of the circle.

South:

I call the watchtower of the South, the spirit of Fire. Element of passion and transformation, help us to make the choices that will lead to greater health and success. Come now and guard our circle. Welcome, and blessed be.

Light a red candle in the South place on the altar, or by the South's point on the edge of the circle.

West:

I call the Watchtower of the West, the spirit of Water. Open our hearts to love, our bodies to healing, and our minds to wisdom from within and without. Come now and guard our circle. Welcome, and blessed be.

Light a blue candle in the West place on the altar, or by the West's point on the edge of the circle.

North:

I call the Watchtower of the North, the spirit of Earth. Nourish and ground us, help us to connect to all the hidden strength inside ourselves. Come now and guard our circle. Welcome, and blessed be.

Light a green candle in the North place on the altar, or by the North's point on the edge of the circle.

HPS invokes the goddess:

Great Goddess, Mother of us all: we your children gather in this circle in your name. Join us here and lend us your power and your wisdom as we practice our Craft. Welcome, and blessed be.

Light a white or silver goddess candle in the middle of the circle or altar.

Sit down and make yourselves comfortable while you share your Books of Shadows. You can go around the circle and take turns showing your books—perhaps discussing the different ways in which you each handle certain elements. (Do you write everything down by hand? Add illustrations? Use mostly spells and ritual components you have found in research books, or make up your own?) You may want to copy a favorite spell or list of ingredients from someone else's book into your own. If any members of your group don't have a Book of Shadows, now is a good time for them to start one. Take as much time with this as you need—your Book of Shadows is an important tool, and this is the perfect opportunity to benefit from the knowledge gathered by the others in your group. Don't forget to have *fun.*

Once you are done sharing out of your own Books, you can create a Book of Shadows for your group. You can decorate this in any way that you want, as long as you all agree. Blue Moon Circle used a large black book with a gold pentacle on the front. On the inside front cover we wrote the name of the group, and everyone signed their names. We glued a piece of paper on the opposite page, on which we had typed out in a fancy font the name of the group, the date, and the following, which you are free to use:

By the powers of Earth, Air, Fire and Water,

With the blessing of the goddess and the god,

For the good of all

And according to the free will of all

In perfect love and perfect trust

So do we practice our Craft.

Since then, we have added every spell and ritual that we have done as a group, as well as pictures of group activities and any other information we thought was important.

If you want, you can pass the Book around the circle and everyone can add a drawing. Or you can take turns taking it home at a later date and adding illustrations, information, or anything else you want to have in this shared tool.

Once you have finished working on your books, you can say the following blessing together. Remember to speak slowly and clearly, and put all your intent behind the words.

BOOK OF SHADOWS BLESSING

Bless this Book in the name of the goddess and the god

Who guide my feet on the Path of Beauty

Let it be filled with wisdom and knowledge

Let me use it only for good

Let me share it with those who need it

Let it help me grow in my Craft

And in my life.

So mote it be.

Note: If you want, you can print out this blessing on a fancy card (we use postcard stock, which is usually just the right size) and glue it into your book after you use it for the ritual. Some Witches believe that everything that goes into your Book of Shadows should be handwritten. As with the rest of your practice, just do what feels right to you.

- Pass cakes and ale.

HPS/HP says:

Bless these cakes, a symbol of Earth's bounty. May they feed our souls as well as our bodies." (You can say to each other as you pass the cakes: "May you never hunger.")

HPS/HP says:

Bless this wine (or juice), fruit of the earth. May it remind us always of the sweetness of life. (You can say to each other as you pass the ale: "May you never thirst.")

- Pass the speaking stick—each person should have a turn to speak uninterrupted of what is in his or her heart.
- Dismiss the quarters: This can be as simple as saying "Power of (Earth, Air, Fire, Water), thank you for guarding our circle. Farewell, and blessed be." Start at North, then do West, South, and finish with East. Snuff out each candle after you dismiss that element. It is considered disrespectful to simply blow out the candles.
- Thank the goddess:

HPS says:

We thank you Gracious Lady of the Moon for your presence in our circle tonight and in our lives. May you continue to watch over us, and lend us your wisdom, grace, and strength. So mote it be. Snuff out goddess candle.

- Open the circle. If you cast the circle hand to hand, you can simply join hands, raise them above your heads, and the HPS should say, "The circle is open but never broken. Merrie meet, merrie part, and merrie meet again." Then let go of each other's hands. Or the HPS can walk counterclockwise around the circle with her athame.

If you like, you can recite the Wiccan Rede together. There are many different versions. This is the one we use most of the time:

the wiccan rede

Bide the Wiccan law ye must

In perfect love, In perfect trust

Eight words the Wiccan Rede fulfill

An it harm none, do as ye will

Lest in thy self defense it be

Ever mind the law of three

Follow this with mind and heart

And merrie ye meet, and merrie ye part."

(We sometimes add: "And merrie meet again.")

January Full Moon

Group dedication ritual

A group dedication is not exactly the same thing as an individual dedication, although they have many of the same components. An individual Witch is either self-dedicated, or dedicated by a High Priest and/or High Priestess, usually the one(s) leading that particular Witch's group. A group dedication is done by the group as a whole.

Since many Witches start out as solitary practitioners, it is fairly common to be self-dedicated. A dedication—no matter how it is done—is basically a declaration that you intend to walk the path of the old gods, and that you vow to follow that path to the best of your abilities.

That sounds pretty simple, and it is. But as with much else that is Wiccan, there is a catch. *You have to mean it.*

When you dedicate yourself, the gods are listening. You need to be sure that you mean what you say, and that you intend to walk this path for the rest of your life, following the rules that Wicca entails. ("Do no harm" and the rest.)

Does this mean that you can never change your mind? Of course not. People can and do decide that this path is not for them after all, and go off to find a different one. What it does mean, however, is that you have to mean it with all your heart at the time you make your dedication.

Think of it like a marriage ceremony—you can change your mind later, but it is expected that you wouldn't be taking those vows unless you really believe at the time you make them that you intend to keep them for the rest of your life.

Does that mean that you can't practice Witchcraft if you aren't sure that you want to do it for the rest of your life? No, not at all. Many Witches practice for years without being dedicated. Some are dedicated right away. The older forms of coven-craft, such as Alexandrian or Gardnerian, actually wouldn't let you be dedicated until you'd practiced for at least a year and a day. That was their way of ensuring that no one took the dedication frivolously. And even after a year and a day, the covener could only be dedicated if the High Priest and Priestess felt that he or she was truly ready.

It is my belief that no one can make the judgment about whether or not you are ready to be dedicated better than you can. Think about it. Ask for guidance if you have any doubts. But the truth is, you will probably know when the time is right. Listen to your "inner voice." It is often your best guide.

The same thing is true for a group dedication. You may want to do one right away. You may want to practice together for a year and a day first, to be sure that you really "fit" together. Only you and your group can decide what is right for you all.

A group dedication, unlike a personal one, is not likely to last for a lifetime. Members come and go—people change, move away, become angry with each other, decide that they are more suited to solitary work, and the like. Still, it is a serious commitment to the gods and to each other, and should not be undertaken lightly.

At the same time, a group dedication is an occasion for joy and even fun. Remember that Wicca is practiced with "reverence and mirth." Be sure that you are ready, be serious in your vows, but don't forget to enjoy the moment, too. Your group is the family that you have chosen. These people, out of all others in the world, are those with whom you will share your Craft, in perfect love and perfect trust. Rejoice in each other, and feel your circle fill up with love and magick!

suppLies:

❏ A small taper candle for each member of the group (you can all use the same color, or you can each have a different color), a large white group candle, toothpicks or sharp sticks to write with, a long piece of red yarn. Optional are a special chalice for group work only, ritual anointing oil, and a box for your yarn to be put into once the ritual is over.

• • •

- Consecrate and cleanse the circle by passing sage or incense.

- Consecrate and cleanse the circle by passing salt and water.

- Cast the circle. This is a powerful and important ritual, so be sure to focus when casting the circle. This is a good time to use the formal casting where the HPS walks around the outside of the circle with her athame or sword. Or you can cast the circle hand to hand.

- Call the quarters

HPS invokes the goddess:

Great Goddess, we your children come before you on this the night of your Full Moon, symbol of your power and beauty. Be with us tonight, and lend us your strength, your wisdom, and your power. Watch over us in this rite, as we dedicate ourselves to each other and to you. Welcome, and blessed be.

HPS:

We have come together tonight for the purpose of dedicating ourselves and this group, _____[name of group]. This rite formalizes our intent to work together as we follow the path of the old gods, and practice our Craft to the best of our abilities. We state our intention to work together in perfect love and perfect trust, for the betterment of all. Are all here so agreed? (All members should answer: "We are.")

Group members can sit for the next part of the ritual.

All members are given a colored candle, which they should inscribe with their names (using their athame, a toothpick, or a stick). They can use their Wiccan name, if they have one, and/or their mundane names. The large white group candle is passed around the circle, and each member can inscribe it with whatever he or she feels is appropriate for the moment—names, symbols, runes, and so forth. The candle can be anointed with a ritual oil if it is available, and then placed back in the center of the circle.

Once this is completed, everyone should stand again. The next part can be performed by the HPS or HP on each member, or you can go around the circle and have each circle or coven member do the next.

Use the red yarn to "take the measure" of each group member. Without cutting the yarn, measure off a length equal to the height of that person (if someone is six feet tall, you would measure off six feet of yarn, so be sure that you have enough yarn when you start.) Tie a knot at that spot, then take the measure of the next member. When you are done, you will have a long piece of yarn with as many knots in it as there are group members. You can then cut it off at the end. This piece of yarn represents your group. You can anoint it with oil if you like, and you may wish to keep it in a special box. Pass it around the circle and let everyone hold it for a moment and put energy into it. In later rituals, you can use this length of yarn to mark out your circle space, if you like, or just keep it someplace safe. (Note: if you add a new member to the group later on, you can measure out a new length for him or her and tie it onto the end of the group piece.)

When you are finished, spread the piece of yarn out around the inside of the circle so that each person is holding onto a knot. It doesn't matter if it is their "own" knot, and there will probably be yarn lying on the floor between each of you, which is fine.

Holding the yarn in their left hands, the members will take their colored candles and light them off the goddess candle. Together, the group members will light the white group candle with their individual candles, then blow out the individual candles, leaving the group candle burning. (This may not go as smoothly as it is written, which is okay. Don't forget to laugh at yourselves and have fun, even if things go wrong.)

With all still standing, the HPS will lead the group in the dedication. If necessary, you can hold the yarn in your left hand, while holding a book or paper with the words in your right:

group dedication

We are Witches

We walk the path of the old gods

From this moment Forth

We will not walk alone

Together, we will worship

Together, we will practice our Craft

Together, we will learn and grow

We vow to work, From this day Forward

In perfect love and perfect trust

According to the Free will of all

And For the good of all

Creating only beauty

Singing in harmony

Our song upon the earth

Love is the law and love is the bond

In the name of the goddess and the god

So do we vow, and so mote it be.

- Take a moment of silence. If you like, you can pass a hug or a kiss around the circle. Sit.
- Pass cakes and ale. These should be something special and, if you want, you can serve whatever you are drinking in a special chalice that will be reserved for the group from that time on.
- Pass the speaking stick.
- Dismiss the quarters.

HPS thanks the goddess:

Great Goddess, Mother of us all, we thank you for your presence in our circle at this ritual of dedication. May you continue to watch over us when we are together, and when we are apart. Farewell, and blessed be.

Open the circle by clasping hands and reciting the Wiccan Rede (see chapter 17), or finish by dropping your hands (one by one or all together) and saying: "The circle is open but never broken."

Notes

CHAPTER 5

feBRuaRy

For most of us in the Northern Hemisphere, February is a cold and gloomy month that falls in the middle of winter. Often, spring seems too far off to imagine. So it may seem ironic that on the second day of February, Wiccans celebrate Imbolc, a holiday dedicated to the beginning of spring.

The explanation for this can be found in the name of the holiday itself. Imbolc, or Imbolg, comes from Celtic origins, and means "in the belly." From what I have read, this name had two meanings. The first refers to the fact that although the ground may be covered with snow, far underneath the earth the earliest beginnings of spring are stirring. The second has to do with an alternative translation, "ewe's milk." In the days when winter was a time of scarcity, the beginning of lambing season signaled the end to the worst of the struggle and deprivation. When the lambs were in their mothers' bellies, there would be milk for a hungry family.

Whichever translation you use, Imbolc is a time of rejoicing. Despite the harsh weather that might be lurking outside our windows, we know that the end is in sight. Far beneath our feet, seeds are beginning to sprout. Under the snow, the first small buds are forming on the trees. It is time to start shaking off the winter doldrums and to begin implementing the plans we made during the calm and quiet of the preceding season.

Imbolc has come down through its pagan traditions into modern life in a new incarnation: Groundhog Day. On that day, the groundhog pokes its head up and predicts how many weeks we must wait until the start of spring. Imbolc serves much the same purpose as that furry psychic—it alerts us that spring is coming and that now is the time to start thinking about the practical applications of our winter dreaming.

Wiccans see this holiday as a time for cleansing and purification. The goddess is changing from Crone to Maiden, and the god is slowly growing from infant into energetic child. It is a time to take our brooms and sweep away all the clutter from our homes, our minds, and our spirits in order to make room for our new goals.

Imbolc is a fire festival, and we use the symbolism of the flames to burn away anything that no longer works for us or that might stand in the way of our making positive changes. Since the Irish celebration of this holiday was dedicated to Brigit (some still call it "Brigit's Day"), a triple goddess of smith-craft, healing, and the arts, it is appropriate to celebrate it in any way that is creative or artistic. It is also considered to be a good time for divination work.

Where I live, a local Wiccan High Priestess leads a yearly Imbolc event that is open to the general public and held at a community location. Her group (which I belonged to for many years) draws a large labyrinth on the floor and people walk the labyrinth one by one as everyone else sits in circle drumming.

As you walk, you ponder the direction your life might take during the coming year, and ask the gods for guidance. When you reach the center of the labyrinth, you reach into the cauldron that is waiting there and pull out a slip of paper. Each piece of paper has a word or phrase on it; usually there are about twenty different choices. (It is a running joke among my friends that I have defied the odds by picking out the word "patience" four years in a row. I'm guessing this means I'm a slow learner . . .)

The ritual is almost entirely silent except for the calling of the quarters, the invoking of the gods, and the drumming during the ritual. This creates a surprisingly powerful and moving experience.

The Imbolc ritual in this chapter is based in part on that experience. I hope you find it helpful as you start out upon the path you will follow in the months to come.

Imbolc ritual

supplies:

❑ Cauldron or bowl filled with sand or sea salt (large enough to put the candles in)

❑ Numerous small white candles (tea lights or votives work fine)

❑ Bowl with slips of paper (write on the slips ahead of time—one word or phrase per slip, at least twice as many slips as you have people, so everyone has a choice. Examples might include "compassion," "courage," "patience," "new beginnings," and the like.)

❑ Broom (preferably one that is kept for magickal use)

• • •

Note: Drums are a must for this ritual. If you don't have one yet, now is a good time to get one. If there are people who don't have drums, you can make do with rattles or clapping, but drumming is best.

You may wish to make your circle larger than usual, to allow people enough space to walk in. Also, you may want to make sure that the people who are calling the quarters know where to stand and what is expected of them.

HPS/HP:

Welcome to our celebration of Imbolc. This holiday celebrates the first stirrings of spring underneath the often frozen ground. It is a time to sweep away the old and welcome in the new. During the slower-paced winter days, we have plotted and planned our goals for the coming year. Now it is time to start implementing those plans.

HPS/HP:

This ritual will be different from the usual pattern. Tonight we will be mostly silent, the better to hear our inner voices and the voices of the gods. We will cast the circle without words, simply using the broom to sweep away negativity and enclose us in safety. We will call the quarters in silence, knowing that they will hear the summons on whatever level we send it out. We will invoke the gods with hearts instead of words.

HPS/HP:

Then we will start drumming. As we drum, we will focus on our plans for the coming year. We will ponder our hopes, our dreams, and any questions we might have about the best way in which to bring those dreams to fruition.

HPS/HP:

One by one, we will walk clockwise around the inside of the circle. Slowly, without speaking, we will walk the sacred space, listening to the drums, the beating of our hearts, and our own inner wisdom. When it is your turn, you may walk for as long as you need, opening yourself to guidance from within and without. When you are ready, stop in front of the bowl on the altar and take out a piece of paper. On that paper, you may find an answer to your questions or a clue as to which path is best for you. Take a moment to look inward and see what that word means to you. Then light a candle in the cauldron of changes, and continue clockwise back to your place in the circle.

HPS/HP:

When we are all finished, we will pass cakes and ale and resume speaking as usual.

- HPS takes the broom and walks around the outside of the circle, sweeping.
- Cleanse and consecrate the circle by passing sage or incense (in silence).
- Cleanse and consecrate the circle by passing salt and water (in silence).
- Circle member turns to East and gestures [point, or draw, a pentacle in the air], all follow suit. The circle member calls the quarters without speaking. Light yellow candle.
- Circle member turns and gestures to the South, all follow suit. Light red candle.

- Circle member turns and gestures to the West, all follow suit. Light blue candle.

- Circle member turns and gestures to the North, all follow suit. Light green candle.

- HP (or HPS) lifts his arms and makes the sign of the Horned God (middle three fingers bent in to palm, thumb and pinky out), all follow suit. HP invokes the god silently, then lights the god candle.

- HPS (or HP) lifts her arms and gestures with palms up to the sky, all follow suit. HPS invokes the goddess silently, then lights the goddess candle.

- HPS/HP start drumming. All drum.

- Participants take turns walking around the circle in silent meditation, then taking a slip of paper and lighting a candle. Drumming continues.

- When everyone has had a turn, the drumming stops. Everyone can relax and take a deep breath.

- Pass cakes and ale (HPS/HP speak cakes and ale blessing as usual)

- Pass the speaking stick. Participants may speak about the word on their slip of paper or not, as they choose. They can also talk about their goals for the coming year.

- Dismiss the quarters (speaking as usual).

HP thanks the god:

Great God, we thank you for helping us to walk our paths, and for sending us wisdom to aid us along the way. May you continue to guide and inspire us from this day forth. So mote it be. (All repeat: "So mote it be.")

HPS thanks the goddess:

Great Goddess, we thank you for sending us clarity and inspiration to help us as we choose our next steps. May your love light our way from this day forth. So mote it be. (All repeat: "So mote it be.")

Open the circle by reciting the Wiccan Rede, or simply by joining hands and saying: "The circle is open but never broken—merrie meet, merrie part, and merrie meet again." Feast!

February New Moon

Tool consecration and blessing

While it is possible to practice Witchcraft with nothing more than your heart, hands, and mind, most Wiccans find it easier (and more fun) to do so with the aid of certain tools. And although no two Witches are likely to own exactly the same equipment, most of us have at least a few of the basics—athame, crystals, tarot cards, drums, chalice, and the like. (See chapter 2 for more detailed information.)

Magickal tools are not like hammers and screwdrivers. They are usually kept together in a special place, and you never loan them to your neighbors. In fact, some Witches believe it is inappropriate for anyone else even to touch your magickal tools. Personally, I don't worry about that much, although I would recommend keeping your tools away from anyone with negative energy.

So what makes your athame different from any of the knives in your kitchen drawer? Obviously, the way it is used—a magickal tool should *only* be used for rituals, and never for mundane purposes. If you have a chalice that is used in circle, for instance, don't drink your wine from it at dinner. And the broom that sweeps the circle clear of negativity should never be used to clean the kitchen floor.

But the difference goes beyond their function. Most magickal tools are also blessed and consecrated for magickal use, adding to their power and their purpose. Consecrating a tool is another way to focus intent—an important element of spellwork. By blessing and consecrating your athame, you are saying to the universe (and to yourself): this tool is a part of my magick, it has power beyond the everyday, and it is an extension of my will.

Blessing and consecrating a tool also reinforces your intention to use that item wisely and only in a positive manner. As you use a particular tool more and more often, it absorbs energy from the work you do and becomes even more powerful.

Witches, shamans, and other magick workers have used special tools in their rituals for as long as recorded human history, and probably before. Tools help to direct and boost energy, provide focus, and aid in creating a ceremonial atmosphere. Most importantly, they are a subconscious signal that tells us: now we are doing magick.

Most of the time, tools only need to be consecrated once, when you first acquire them. Occasionally a tool will require re-consecration, usually because it was somehow exposed to negative energy. (Your creepy neighbor wanders over to your altar and picks up your athame, for instance, and afterwards it just doesn't feel right.)

If you acquire a tool from an unknown source or get a hand-me-down from someone whose energy you are not quite sure of, it is often a good idea to do a little extra cleansing before the actual consecration. Tools can be cleansed by leaving them out for a night under the light of the Full Moon (this is especially good for crystals), or by holding them under running water.

The ritual in this chapter is good for when your group has a number of items to be consecrated, but the tool blessing can be used at any time for individual tools as well.

supplies:

These are all items that are normally on the altar table for most rituals anyway, but if you don't use them for your group rituals on a regular basis, here is a list:

- ❏ Sea salt in a small bowl
- ❏ Water in a small bowl (water from a well or stream is best; the water should be as pure as possible)
- ❏ Sage or incense
- ❏ Candle (you may use the goddess candle or any of the quarter candles for this)
- ❏ Optional: a medium/large feather

Note: You may also want to consecrate larger amounts of salt and a container of water for use in future rituals, although this is not strictly necessary. If you are just starting out, you may even want to consecrate the altar table itself.

• • •

- • Consecrate and cleanse the circle with sage or incense
- • Consecrate and cleanse the circle with salt and water

- Cast the circle hand to hand or by having the HPS walk around the outside of the circle with her athame or sword
- Call the quarters
- HPS invokes the goddess

Sit comfortably in the circle. Each circle member can show the others the tools that they have brought to be consecrated. It is fine to pass them around the circle if you want, and to share any interesting stories you might have about how you acquired them. It can be particularly interesting to compare the pictures on different decks of tarot cards. This is the perfect time to gift someone else in your group with a tool if you have an extra one or if you've bought one for that purpose. Some Witches believe that all your tools should be a gift from someone else and that you should never buy them for yourself. This seems pretty impractical to me, but it is nice to get one or two in this way, if that is how it works out.

The group should decide how they want to do the consecration and blessing—all of the tools all at once, all of the same type of tool (athames) at the same time, all of one person's tools at one time, or each individual tool one at a time. There is no wrong way; the end result is exactly the same. Make the decision based on how the group feels and how many tools there are to be blessed—and then go from there.

If you are doing all the tools at once, you can read the blessing together, and substitute "these tools" for "this athame" (or whatever the tools is) on the first line, and "they" for "it" in the following lines. The actions taken during the blessing can be done by the HPS or HP for everyone, or each member can do his or her own.

The way it is written here is for individual tool blessing or to be read in unison by the group. If the HPS does the blessing for someone else, substitute the words "her" or "his" for "my":

tool consecration and blessing

Great Goddess, bless this _____

That it may be used for good and never harm

That it may help me in my Craft

And aid me in my magickal work

From this day Forward

May it be blessed and consecrated

By the power of Earth (sprinkle with salt)

By the power of Air (waft with feather, incense or sage)

By the power of Fire (pass over candle or through flame if fireproof)

And by the power of Water (sprinkle with water)

And by the power of the Spirit which lies within us all

So mote it be

• • •

After all the tools are consecrated, take a moment of silence, and visualize yourselves using them in future rituals with powerful results.

- Pass cakes and ale
- Pass the speaking stick
- Dismiss the quarters
- HPS thanks the goddess
- Open the circle

February Full Moon

Peace and happiness oil

Magickal oils are another tool that can often be found among a knowledgeable Witch's supplies. They are often used to anoint the participants in a ritual and can be used to anoint many of the ritual components such as candles and charms as well.

They add power and focus to a spell in two primary ways. First, since essential oils are created using large amounts of herbs and flowers, they absorb much of the natural energy from the plants. That energy (which differs depending on which plants are used) is then passed on to the person or object on which the magickal oil is placed.

Second, of all our five (or six) senses, the sense of smell is the most connected to memory and emotion. Just as the smell of an apple pie being baked may instantly bring you back to your grandmother's kitchen, the smell of a magickal oil can generate a deep and powerful subconscious response. When you use sage to cleanse your circle every time you meet, your mind recognizes the smell and automatically sends you into the proper mental state. If you use a magickal oil often enough, the smell alone can help to boost the power of the spells with which you use it.

Magickal oils are created using various essential oils and one or more base oils. All of these should be of the best quality that you can find and afford, since the power of the finished oil is dependent on the power of the ingredients you put into it. This doesn't mean that you have to sell the family silver in order to have good magickal oils; thankfully, many basic essential oils are both readily available and reasonably priced.

A few exceptions, like chamomile and rose, can be quite pricey. However, they are so effective and so useful that you may wish to purchase small amounts and use them only when they are most needed. I try not to use the really hard-to-find essential oils in my spells, but if you can only find four out of the five ingredients (for example), the spell should work perfectly well anyway. If at all possible, do not use perfume oils. Unlike essential oils, these are artificial scents—and while they are much cheaper, they may not have the same effect as the real thing.

Essential oils can be found at most health food, New Age, and pagan shops, as well as online. There can be vast differences in quality from one company to the next, so you may have to experiment or ask for the advice of someone who has experience if you haven't bought essential oils before. Price is not necessarily an indication of quality; I like the Natural Alchemy line, which is quite reasonable.

Base oils can be anything from extra-virgin olive oil from your kitchen cabinet to body oils like sesame, grapeseed, or jojoba. Keep in mind that all base oils will go rancid eventually. Adding a little Vitamin E may help, but it is probably best to make up only small amounts at a time and create a new batch as necessary.

Please remember that most essential oils and all magickal oils should only be used topically, and should not be ingested. If you use them directly on your skin or in a bath, be cautious if you have any plant allergies.

As with all things magickal, ingredients that have been grown and harvested with your own hands are the most powerful. If you so desire, you can make herbal oils using plants from your own garden— but don't worry if you don't have the time, space, or inclination to do so. There are many perfectly good magickal oils available in Wiccan stores and catalogs, and it is easy and fun to use purchased essential oils, like those in the peace and happiness oil on the following pages.

suppLies:

❏ Bergamot essential oil

❏ Chamomile essential oil

❏ Geranium essential oil

❏ Lavender essential oil

❏ Lemon balm essential oil

❏ Base oil, such as sesame oil or a good olive oil

❏ Small glass or plastic vials or bottles (glass is preferable), with lids and/or dropper tops (one for each person in the group)

❏ Optional: extra droppers if the bottles of essential oil don't have them. (Don't use the same dropper for more than one oil if you can avoid it.)

❏ Optional: labels that say "Peace & Happiness Oil." (You will want to label them in some way so that you know what it is later, but it is up to you how simple or fancy you wish to make these labels.)

Note: If you can't find one or more of the essential oils, you can substitute an extra drop or two of one of the others. It is best to have at least four of the five oils if you can, and you must have at least three. If you can't find one of the oils on the list above, you can substitute rose or lemon.

•   •   •

- Consecrate and cleanse the circle with sage or incense.
- Consecrate and cleanse the circle with salt and water.
- Cast the circle hand to hand.
- Call the quarters.
- HPS invokes the goddess (Full Moon invocation—see chapter 17.)
- Sit down and make yourselves comfortable.
- Start by filling each individual vial about three quarters full with the base oil.
- Then pass the essential oils around the circle one by one. The HPS can tell what each one is used for, or each circle member can tell about one in turn. After each oil is named and described, it should be passed around the circle, and the required number of drops placed in each individual vial.

  › Bergamot—two drops—peace, happiness, restful sleep
  › Chamomile—one drop—sleep, meditation, peace
  › Geranium—two drops—happiness, protection
  › Lavender—two drops—health, love, peace
  › Lemon Balm—two drops—peace, money, purification

(Note that there are nine drops total. Nine is a powerful magickal number. The HPS may mention this.)

- When the oils are finished, cap the vial and swirl gently nine times in a clockwise motion to mix. Label the bottles containing your final mixture.
- Then consecrate and bless the oil using the tool consecration and blessing spell from the New Moon earlier this month:

tooL consecration and blessing spell

Great Goddess, bless this oil

That it may be used for good and never harm

That it may help me in my Craft

And aid me in my magickal work

From this day forward

May it be blessed and consecrated

By the power of Earth

By the power of Air

By the power of Fire

And by the power of Water

And by the power of the Spirit which lies within us all

So mote it be

• • •

(The oil may be kept on your altar or another safe space—it will be used in many future rituals. You can also place a drop on your forehead or over your heart any time you feel the need.)

- Pass cakes and ale.
- Pass the speaking stick.
- Dismiss the quarters.
- HPS thanks the goddess.
- Open the circle.

✺ Notes

_____   _____
_____   _____
_____   _____
_____   _____
_____   _____
_____   _____
_____   _____
_____   _____
_____   _____
_____   _____
_____   _____
_____   _____
_____   _____
_____   _____
_____   _____
_____   _____
_____   _____

march

March is kind of a rough month here in Upstate New York where I live. By then, winter has been around for a really long time. Everywhere you look there are piles of dirty snow, stark leafless trees, and cold, grumpy people. It seems as if winter will never end.

And then the first crocus peeks its head up, and you notice buds coming out on the forsythia bushes. The days get longer and lighter, and it suddenly occurs to you that warm weather might really come again.

The Spring Equinox, which falls on or around March twenty-first, is truly a time for celebration. For the first time since the Autumn Equinox, there is a perfect balance between night and day, and we are moving into a time of increased light and energy. We rejoice at the return of the Maiden Goddess in all her exuberant, youthful glory, and we know that along with spring she brings to us the gift of endless possibility.

This holiday represents new life and new growth. We celebrate by decorating eggs (which represent fertility), drinking pomegranate juice, and making plans for the year to come.

This is the time to finally let go of any old patterns that might be getting in the way of your living your life to the fullest, and concentrate on maximizing your growth as both a Witch and as a human being.

Spring Equinox ritual

For many of us, it is still too cold to celebrate the Spring Equinox outside. This ritual is designed to be performed indoors. If you are lucky enough to be able to do it outside, just skip the part about walking through the curtains.

supplies:

❑ Two curtains or large pieces of cloth: one white (sheets work fine), one flowered.

❑ A bell or gong.

❑ Seed packets (enough for everyone in your circle to get two or three, unless it is a large circle, in which case one each is good): twenty to thirty total.

❑ Slips of paper to attach to seed packets (write on each a different way to grow: see the list at end of this ritual): one for each packet.

❑ Oil for anointing.

Note: You can decorate your altar with fresh flowers and decorated eggs. We used chocolate malted eggs that looked like robin eggs . . . fun, and you can eat them when you're done!

• • •

- All gather in an outer room.

- Circle member sits in an inner room with a bell. (At my house, the dining room was the "outer room" and the living room was the "inner room," but you can gather in any space large enough to hold your group and move to any space large enough for the ritual.)

- One by one, participants walk toward the two curtains that have been hung in the doorway (the first one white, the second one with a floral print). HPS or HP pulls back the white curtain and says: "Pass from winter into spring, and blessed be," then pulls back the flowered curtain so that each participant can enter the next room.

- As people enter the room, a circle member anoints them with oil, saying: "Enter into this sacred space, and blessed be."

- The circle member already in the room rings the altar bell as each person enters. (This is to signal that they have moved into a sacred space.)
- Once in circle, participants drum quietly until everyone has entered the circle. (If you have a large group attending, it is not a bad idea to have a circle member go in first and start drumming to set an example)
- HPS or HP enters last, is anointed, and then anoints the circle member who anointed her or him. Drumming stops, and all stand.

HPS:

Welcome to our celebration of the Spring Equinox, also known as Ostara. This is a time of hope and renewal, growth and rebirth. As the Wheel of the Year turns again to bring us out of the darkness of winter, and into the light of spring, we are given the chance to start fresh, and welcome new energy into our lives.

- Pass sage to consecrate and cleanse the circle.
- Pass salt and water around the circle.

HPS/HP casts circle (walks around circle with athame):

I cast the circle round and round, from Earth to Sky, from Sky to Ground. I conjure now this sacred place, outside time, and outside space. The circle is cast, we are between the worlds.

- Call the quarters.

HPS/HP invokes god and goddess:

Great Goddess, Bright Maiden, Lady of the Growing Things, bless our circle with your presence as we celebrate the coming of spring. Lend us your wisdom and your grace as you help us to grow to our full potential. Welcome, and blessed be.

Great God, Green Man, Lord of the Wild Things, bless our circle with your presence as we celebrate the coming of spring. Lend us your strength and your determination, and help us to become all that we wish ourselves to be. Welcome, and blessed be.

HPS:

Spring is a time of growth. Not just for the grass and trees, but for us as well. Tonight we turn our energy and the energy of this circle to the goal of growing in all the positive and beneficial ways available to us. In this circle, our intent is focused, our power immeasurable. And together, we can invoke positive change, not only in our own lives, but in the world surrounding us.

- Pass a bowl filled with slips of paper that are attached to seed packets. Each person should take a seed packet, read the slip out loud, and pass the bowl to the next person. The HPS starts. (Examples: "May we grow in spirit." "May we grow in health." "May we grow in . . . [prosperity, wisdom, courage, faith, love, community, forgiveness, power, joy, openness].") When the bowl has gone around once or twice (depending on the size of the circle), the HPS finishes by saying: "May we grow in peace. So mote it be."

HPS/HP or circle member leads meditation (should be read slowly and calmly):

Close your eyes. Take a slow deep breath. Feel the peace of the circle surround you. Take another slow breath and let go of the tensions of the everyday world. These things have no place here. Here there is only calm, and silence and love.

Listen to the slow breathing of those around you. If you listen carefully, you can hear the breathing of the earth as she awakens. The birds call. The trees rustle. The earth stirs.

Send your awareness down. Down through the floor, down beneath the house. Move into the earth. Feel the roots of the trees shifting deep within the earth. Feel the small, subtle stirrings of the bulbs and seeds. They have lain dormant all winter, storing their energy, waiting for their time to grow and blossom."

Now that time has come. All around us, the earth is coming back to life—rising, stretching, growing. Reach out for that energy. Feel it with all your senses—full of potential, unlimited, positive, and powerful.

Open your whole self to this beneficial energy. Let yourself be filled to overflowing with the potential for change and growth, health, prosperity, abundance, and joy.

Send gratitude out to our Mother the earth for this gift, and feel yourself filled with the bountiful energy of spring. Feel yourself begin to blossom and grow, and know that all things are possible.

- Take a moment of silence, then start drumming to wake up the earth and get that energy flowing; if you want, you can do a chant. ("She changes everything she touches" is a particularly good one for this ritual. See chapter 17 for more chants.)

- When drumming has reached its peak, take the energy deep within, and send what is left out into the universe. Ground any excess energy by putting your hands on the floor and sending it down into the earth.

- Pass cakes and ale. Pomegranate juice is perfect for this ritual, because of its associations with the myth of Persephone; deviled eggs or seed cakes are good, too.

- Pass the speaking stick—each person can talk about how they want to grow, or mention some practical plans for self-improvement.

- Dismiss the quarters.

- Thank the god and goddess.

- Open the circle.

- Have a feast! Don't forget to include spring food and your decorated eggs, if you have them.

Here is a list of "May we grow..." suggestions (see page 74) for the slips of paper. Feel free to come up with your own:

May we grow in . . .

Spirit	Openness	Passion	Prosperity	Acceptance
Forgiveness	Courage	Knowledge	Beauty	Love
Compassion	Honesty	Community	Serenity	Creativity
Health	Enthusiasm	Wisdom	Energy	Faith
Potential	Joy	Tolerance	Strength	Power

March New Moon

Banishing ritual

Spring is a time for growth, and for moving forward. But sometimes there are things in our lives—or in ourselves—that get in the way of forward movement and our ability to achieve our goals. The March New Moon is the perfect time to get rid of some of those roadblocks by using a banishing spell.

Banishing spells are fairly simple, really. Instead of asking the gods to help you bring something into your life (prosperity, health, love, and so on), you are asking them to help you to get rid of whatever it is that stands in your way. Decrease as opposed to increase, if you will.

The same principles apply, however. If you want to get rid of something (whether it is extra pounds, self-doubt, debt, loneliness, fear, or negative influences in your life), you first have to be specific and focused in your intent, and then you have to follow up with appropriate actions in your everyday life.

If you want to lose weight, for instance, doing the spell will help you to have willpower and maybe a more realistic self-image. It won't, however, make it so that you magically don't gain weight if you eat an entire chocolate cake. Sorry. (Really, really sorry. I *like* chocolate cake.)

As you prepare to do this spell, remember to figure out exactly what it is that you want (do you really want to lose twenty pounds, or do you just want to feel better about yourself at your current weight?), and then come up with some concrete plans for how you will help the gods to help you achieve your goals.

At the same time, be prepared for the unexpected. Sometimes, after a ritual, you suddenly get an idea for a great new approach to a problem that never occurred to you before; that is one of the ways in which spells work. They also sometimes give you exactly what you asked for in completely unexpected ways, so be sure you really want whatever it is, and be careful how you ask. For instance, if you ask to lose weight, make sure that you specify "in a healthy way." After all, you don't want to drop ten pounds because you got seriously ill.

You don't necessarily have to be specific in the wording of your requests. Just be focused in your intent when you do the spell.

Banishing spell

supplies:

❑ Pencils and slips of paper

❑ A small cauldron or fire-safe bowl

• • •

- Consecrate and cleanse the circle by passing sage.
- Consecrate and cleanse the circle by passing salt and water.
- Cast the circle (hand to hand or by having the HPS/HP walk around the outside of the circle with her/his athame or sword.)
- Call the quarters.

HPS invokes the goddess:

Great Goddess, you who watch over our lives throughout the changing seasons, be with us in our circle tonight as we perform this rite in your name. Lend us your wisdom and your power as you help us to make the choices that will create positive changes in our lives. Welcome, and blessed be.

- Sit in a circle. The HPS should explain the purpose of tonight's ritual:

Tonight we gather to banish those things in our lives that hold us back from growth and happiness. Sometimes such things come from the outside—for instance, an unproductive job or negative influences from others. Sometimes they come from inside of us—like lack of self-confidence, poor judgment, or unhealthy habits.

Either way, if these things are still with us, it is often because we chose—on some level—to allow them to be. Think about the issues you face. Is there some way in which these things serve a purpose in your life? Are you truly ready to let them go?

Gather up your strength of will, and choose those problems that it is time to banish from your life. [Pass around slips of paper and pencils.] Write them down on these slips of paper, while concentrating all your will on your intent to banish them from your life. You can choose to focus on one issue or many; it is up to you. Just be certain you are willing to work on the problem in practical ways once you are outside this magickal space—for even with the help of the gods, we must still help ourselves.

- Take some silent time to have each member think and write.

- When everyone is ready, light a small fire in your cauldron or bowl. You can use a candle or two instead of fire, if you are going to be inside.

The HPS or HP should say:

Great Goddess, we come to you in the darkening of the moon to ask for your blessing and your help. Just as the earth now casts off the chill of winter that held her rigid and unmoving, so we wish to cast off all those things that would hold us back in our lives. And just as you send the soft rains of spring to wash away the ravages of winter, so we ask that you rain down your love upon us to wash away our pain and misfortune. May our troubles vanish with the smoke that carries them to you. So mote it be. [All repeat: "So mote it be."]

- Each circle member takes a turn putting his or her slip of paper into the fire. If they can, they should say out loud what it is they are banishing. (If necessary, it can be said silently if there is something that someone is uncomfortable sharing.) Go around the circle as many times as is necessary. Be careful when burning paper! It's a good idea to have some water handy, just in case. Or you can save the slips of paper and bury or burn them outside later.

- Everyone should stand up and say this spell while walking counterclockwise (widdershins) around the circle. (Almost all movement around the circle is done in a clockwise motion; banishing work is one of the few exceptions.)

BANISHING SPELL

Banish stress and banish sorrow

Banish pain and banish woe

Banish illness, banish fear

As widdershins around we go

Banish tears and loneliness

Banish doubts about our worth

Banish all that's negative

As widdershins we pace the earth

Banish troubles from all others

Banish habits that do harm

Banish lack and banish need

As widdershins we speak this charm

• • •

- Sit and ground (by putting your hands on the floor—or on the ground if you are outside—to let go of any excess energy). Take a moment of silence to let the new balance settle in.

- Pass cakes and ale.

- Pass the speaking stick.

- Dismiss the quarters.

- HPS thanks the goddess and opens the circle.

March Full Moon

Blessing of the Seeds ritual

Seeds are a perfect symbol for Wicca. They represent the very essence of nature, and embody the potential for future growth that is so central to Wiccan practices. Some people believe that seeds contain all the energy of the plants that will eventually spring from them, making them an ideal component in magickal use.

In early spring, the Wheel has turned around again from the time of rest to the start of the time of growth. Those of us who are gardeners start thinking about what we will plant this year, and eagerly await the chance to begin digging. And everyone is watching for the first signs of spring.

The emerging buds and returning birds are a signal to us to start planning our own growth for the coming year. In a sense, we are all our most important gardens. And now that we have cleared out the old useless weeds, we can come together under the light of the Full Moon and plant the seeds for all that we will achieve during the year ahead.

The Blessing of the Seeds ritual serves two purposes. For those who will be growing herbs and other plants for magickal use, this ritual gives us the chance to get them off to a strong magickal start. Even those Witches who don't have gardens can take advantage of this by planting a few herbs in pots indoors.

And as we bless and consecrate the actual seeds used during the ritual, we also bless and consecrate the seeds of our own personal growth. This is the perfect time to decide which areas in your life need the most work this year, and concentrate on planting the seeds for positive change.

suppLies:

❏ Seed packets: preferably seeds for plants with magickal uses, like many herbs and flowers. Vegetable seeds are okay too, especially if you saved seeds from plants you grew last year.

❏ A bowl to put the seed packets in.

• • •

- Consecrate and cleanse the circle by passing sage or incense.
- Consecrate and cleanse the circle by passing salt and water.
- Cast the circle hand to hand.
- Call the quarters.
- HPS invokes the goddess (Full Moon invocation).
- If desired, HPS reads *The Charge of the Goddess*.

The group should sit comfortably. Going around the circle, each member should take a turn discussing the changes that they intend to make in the coming year, and some of the ways in which they plan to bring about those changes. (Examples of things you might want to grow include health, prosperity, love, a less stressful life, and so on.)

Remember that this is only the start of the time for growth. People can still be figuring out what they want to do, and you can help each other to weed through the various ideas that come up, and to decide which are the most important or the most possible to achieve. You are only trying to start the seeds during this ritual; the actual work will come later. This part of the ritual will probably take much longer than the actual magick work, and that's fine. Helping each other to focus and hone intent is an important function of working in a group.

- When you are done discussing your goals for the year, the seeds should be passed around the circle, and everyone should take a packet or two. (You are actually going to plant these seeds, so try to take something that you will want to tend.)
- Holding the seed packets, recite the blessing spell together:

Blessing of the Seeds Spell

Under the moon so full and bright

We conjure up the Lady's light

Love, and warmth and energy

To set the seeds within us free

Bless these seeds that we'll soon sow

Make them strong so they might grow

Full of magick, full of power

Bless them in this moonlit hour

Earth and Water, Air and Fire

Grant us that which we desire

As above and as below

Bless these seeds and help them grow

So mote it be

• • •

Take a moment of silence. Focus on whatever it is that you wish to achieve, and think about those things growing along with the seeds that you will plant. Visualize the tiny green shoots emerging from the ground, growing taller and stronger with every passing day. See the mature plant, vigorous and full of energy, and see yourself succeeding at all the goals that you have set forth. Remember that time is an illusion—the past, the present and the future are all part of a greater whole—and know in your heart that you have already succeeded!

- Take a deep breath and come back to the circle.
- Pass cakes and ale (some kind of cake with seeds in or on it would be appropriate.)
- Pass the speaking stick.
- Dismiss the quarters.
- HPS thanks the goddess.
- Open the circle.

@ Notes

CHAPTER 7

APRIL

@

April is the month when we begin to feel spring in full force. Just as it is a time of transition and growth in nature, so spring is a time for transition and growth in our lives. As Witches, we can take advantage of the natural energy for change that is in the air around us, using it to help us make positive changes in our lives.

At New Moon, the group can discuss change: what in your life is standing in the way of making positive changes, and what you can do to get rid of those patterns that no longer work for your benefit. Many behaviors and personal tendencies can fall into this category, such as unhealthy eating habits, lack of organization or focus, or continuing to take part in a job or relationship despite the unhappiness it brings.

Group members can help each other to pinpoint those habits, which drain energy without giving anything back. Sometimes it is easier to see important issues from the outside. But remember that people can really only make productive changes when they are truly ready to do so. Be supportive and encouraging, but don't push too hard. All things come in their own time. It's okay to start small.

The magick in this chapter is in two parts: the work you do at New Moon helps to set the stage for the work you do at Full Moon. At New Moon, the group will do a spiritual spring cleaning to get rid of the old useless stuff we all carry around. This makes room for the "rebirthing" that takes place at Full Moon.

The April Moon is often known as the Phoenix Moon. The phoenix was a mythical bird that repeatedly went through a cycle of death and rebirth, burning up at the end of its life and then being reborn from its own ashes—the perfect symbol for change and rebirth. This makes April the optimum time for this work. Visualize yourself as a phoenix, and use the fires of Wicca to burn away the things in your life that stand in the way of your rebirth as a stronger, wiser, happier, and more productive you.

April New Moon

Spiritual Spring Cleaning

Supplies:

❏ Cauldron or large bowl filled with sand

❏ Pieces of sage (preferably white sage—it burns best, and you can buy a large smudge stick and break off some individual pieces)

❏ Bowl of water, plus the usual circle candles and other supplies.

Note: In magick, we often use tools and symbols to give our work more focus and power. This spell is a perfect example of the way Wiccans do this. For instance, when you say in the spell "I burn away trouble, turmoil and strife," you also burn a piece of sage to represent the burning away of those aspects from your life. Remember to visualize and focus your energy on the action and on the end result you are hoping to bring about.

• • •

- Cleanse and consecrate the circle space by passing sage or incense. Take this time to quiet your inner self, and put aside the cares of your mundane life. Everyone should begin to quiet down now and focus on the work ahead.

- Pass water and salt.

- Cast the circle. You can do this hand to hand, or by having the High Priestess walk around the outside of the circle with her athame or sword.

- Call the quarters, beginning with East (Air).

- HPS invokes the goddess (Isis or Athena would be good for this ritual, if you want to call her by name).

- Go around the circle and name the things you each want to throw out during this spiritual "spring cleaning." *Be as specific as possible.* For instance, don't just say "bad habits." Instead, say

"Eating junk food after dinner" or "Feeling like I am not good enough". Go around the circle as many times as it takes for everyone to name all the things they intend to give up. Really feel your intention to let go of these things as you say them out loud. Remember that words have power and that focused intent is the first step in bringing about a new reality.

- Drum or clap quietly to raise power. When you are ready, recite the spell together while going through the matching actions described below the spell.

spiritual spring cleaning spell

I burn away trouble, turmoil, and strife [1]

And welcome new blessings into my life

I blow away poverty, debt, and despair [2]

And ask that my days be joyful and fair

I wash away illness, pain, and fatigue [3]

And make more room for the things that I need

I send all my troubles deep into the earth [4]

And make new my life at this time of rebirth.

Chant three times: "Isis, Astarte, Diana, Hecate, Demeter, Kali, Inanna."

• • •

- [1] Place sage in candle flame to set it on fire.
- [2] Blow on sage.
- [3] Wash sage through bowl of water.
- [4] Bury sage in cauldron of sand.

- Take a moment of silence to let the work resonate and sink in.

- Pass cakes and ale.

- Pass the speaking stick. This is a good time to talk about the practical ways you will change your behavior in order to bring about the positive changes you discussed before doing the spell. (For example, if you said you wanted to lose ten pounds, you might state your intention to go to the gym twice a week and eat one cup of ice cream instead of two.)

- Dismiss the quarters.

- HPS thanks the goddess.

- Open the circle, and go back out into the mundane world feeling lighter, freer, and ready to follow up on your magickal work tonight.

April Full Moon

Phoenix Moon ritual

suppLies:

- ❑ Clay
- ❑ Seeds
- ❑ Toothpicks
- ❑ Bowl of water and paper towels for cleaning hands
- ❑ Optional: tape of background music

• • •

- Cleanse and consecrate the circle by passing sage or incense.
- Cleanse and consecrate the circle by passing salt and water.
- Cast the circle hand to hand.
- Call the quarters.
- HPS invokes goddess (Full Moon invocation—see chapter 17).
- Go around the circle and discuss rebirth: what things people want to change, or add into their lives; what practical steps they are taking or intend to take in order to make these things come about.
- The focus here should be on bringing in or adding to your life, instead of letting things go as you did during New Moon. If someone is trying to let go of unhealthy patterns, such as smoking or eating badly, then they should have practical plans to change the behaviors, as well as doing the spell to help them succeed.
- If you did "Spiritual Spring Cleaning" during the last New Moon, discuss how it has affected each of you.

- Put on background music—drumming, or something calm and rhythmic, to get people into the right mood. Hand around balls of clay, and have a bowl of flower seeds in the middle of the altar/table where everyone can reach the seeds. Give everyone a toothpick to use to put features on their clay figure if they want to.

- Have everyone shape their clay, without speaking, into a figure that represents them (female for women, male for men, with as much or as little detail as they want to add). While they work, each person should concentrate on visualizing his or her perfect self: see the changes happening, see what they wish to come into their lives already there. When the figure is done, see it surrounded with a glowing light—made up of will and intent, the goddess's love, the power of the universe. If they want, people can press flower seeds into the clay (either randomly, or in a pattern).

- When everyone is ready, say the spell together:

fuLL mooN speLL foR RebiRth

Goddess bless this perfect me

Make me all I want to be

Help me strive, and then succeed

Give me all the help I need

Healthy, happy, balanced, whole

Body, spirit, heart, and soul

As open as the sky above

Fill my heart with perfect love

As fertile as the earth below

So my dreams shall grow and grow

Healthy, happy, balanced, whole
Body, spirit, heart, and soul

In the East the winds arise
Make me healthy, strong, and wise
In the South the fires gleam
Send prosperity's endless stream

Healthy, happy, balanced, whole
Body, spirit, heart, and soul

In the West the waters flow
As these gifts you do bestow
In the North our steady Earth
Protect us as we now rebirth

Healthy, happy, balanced, whole
Body, spirit, heart, and soul

We thank the gods whose gifts are great
We laugh with joy and celebrate!
So mote it be.

• • •

- Have a moment of silence while you absorb the energy of the spell, and then ground.

- Pass cakes and ale. You could use something like hard-boiled eggs or seed cakes to represent birth and renewal, or spring fruits such as strawberries. Fruit juice, mead, or strawberry wine might be suitable for the drink.

- Pass the speaking stick. If you want, you can use this time to show each other the figures you have made.

- Dismiss the quarters.

- HPS thanks the goddess.

- Open the circle. (If you want, recite the Wiccan Rede.)

Note: Later, if so desired, you can take your figure outside and bury it—in your garden, if you have one, or in a planter, or in a wild place where you go from time to time (you may want to do this right away, under the light of the Full Moon.) Or you can put it on your altar, so that it can remind you of your intention to bring positive changes into your life.

@ Notes

CHAPTER 8

may

@

May is one of my favorite months. Spring has firmly settled in, and we are surrounded by greenery and blooming flowers once again. The days are longer and lighter, and the whole world seems to be coming back to life.

Beltane (also spelled *Beltaine*), or May Day, is also one of my favorite Wiccan holidays. It falls on the first of May, although many Pagans start their celebrations the night before. Based on an ancient Celtic fire festival (the word "Beltane" is derived from the word for "bright fire" in Old Irish), Beltane is the celebration of life and fertility, and marks the beginning of the summer growing season.

Beltane is the time when the goddess and god are at the height of their youth and vigor. The goddess and her consort come together in passion, and renew the earth with their love. Pagans have traditionally celebrated this season with dancing, feasting, and all acts sensual and sexual. It is the perfect time for handfasting (the pagan marriage ritual), for love spells, and for magick dealing with increase of any kind.

Wiccans dance around the Maypole (the pole represents the god, and the colored ribbons represent the goddess winding herself around him in love and union), jump the fire, and celebrate love in all its forms.

Pagan partners, whether long term or temporary, come together in the Great Rite. This magickal sexual ritual uses the participants' own bodies to symbolically represent the coming together of goddess and god in a powerful form of worship. Or Witches wander through the woods alone, reveling in nature (and picking up trash along the way).

No matter how they celebrate, this is a time for Wiccans to gather with others with like beliefs and renew our commitments to the ancient gods, to the land, and to each other. So light the bonfire, dance around the Maypole, sing, drum, and feast. Rejoice in the company of other Witches, and in the power and glory that it is Wicca.

Beltane ritual

Notes: Unlike many Wiccan rituals, Beltane is usually celebrated during the day (sometimes all day and into the night!) If at all possible, this ritual should take place outside around a bonfire. I would rather celebrate a day early or late if it rains, for instance, if waiting means that we can be outside rather than inside.

Remember to make the bonfire fairly small if you are planning on jumping it—nobody wants to repeat the Burning Times by mistake! Or you can jump over a small fire in a bowl or cauldron, or a candle instead, and save the bonfire for dancing around. It is a good idea to have a bucket of water standing by, just in case.

If you are going to use a Maypole, you can cut down a small tree (this is typically the men's job, while the women dig the hole for it—no sexual symbolism there, eh?), or simply find a medium-sized pole to stick into the ground. Tie multicolored ribbons around the top, and dance in opposite directions around the pole, weaving the ribbons in and out as you go.

As an alternative, you can use a "May bush" instead. Pick a living bush or tree on the property you will be using for your ritual, and take turns tying a ribbon around a branch while making a wish. This is sometimes easier for small groups to do, when there aren't enough people to do a real Maypole dance. If you have to be inside, you can even use a tall houseplant!

The Beltane ritual in this chapter has many of these different elements—you can do them all, or leave some out if you choose. For instance, the ritual uses the May bush, but feel free to do the Maypole dance instead, if you have enough room and enough people.

If you want, you can cast the circle as usual. But one of the large Beltane gatherings I've been to locally does things somewhat differently for this holiday. Due to the greater number of participants (there are sometimes over one hundred people there) and the wide-ranging activities, some of which require a lot of space, the Beltane ritual is done using what is referred to as an "open circle." In this instance, the circle is mentally and spiritually expanded to include the entire surroundings, and the whole world. The truly amazing amount of positive energy generated by the ritual itself is enough to create sacred space and keep us safe, even without the formal circle casting.

supplies:

These will vary depending on which parts of the ritual you decide to do, and how you decide to do them. The supply list covers everything you might need. Just leave out anything you decide not to use.

❑ Wood for a bonfire (pre-dig the fire pit if you don't have one, or use a portable fire pit)

❑ And/or a small cauldron or large dish with coals, and an alcohol fire or candles

❑ A Maypole (or pick out a bush to use as a May bush)

❑ Many multicolored ribbons (these should be longer than your pole, as they get shorter as you wind around)

❑ Copies of *The Charge of the Goddess* and *The Charge of the God* (see the last section of this book)

❑ Mead or juice

❑ Flowers to decorate the altar

• • •

• Consecrate and cleanse the circle by having a group member walk around the outside with sage or incense. (Rose or mint incenses are good.) Waft with a feather if you like.

• Consecrate and cleanse the circle by having a group member walk around the outside with salt and/or water. (You can do these separately if you want.)

• If doing so, cast the circle by having the HPS or HP walk around the outside of the circle with an athame or sword.

• Call the quarters.

HP invokes the god:

Great Pan, Lord of the Woods and King of the Wild Creatures, come dance with us on this magickal day! We gather here to rejoice in love and light and to celebrate your union. Be with us in this sacred space! Fill our minds and hearts and spirits! Welcome, Green Man, and blessed be!

HPS invokes the goddess:

Great Rhiannon, Lady of the Fertile Fields and Queen of the Fairies, come sing with us on this magickal day! We are here to rejoice in love and laughter and to celebrate your transformation from Maiden to Mother. Be with us in this sacred space! Fill our minds and hearts and spirits! Welcome, Queen of the May, and blessed be!

- HPS reads *The Charge of the Goddess*.
- HP (or another circle member / guest) reads *The Charge of the God*.

HPS/HP:

We are gathered here to celebrate Beltane, also known as May Day. Passed down to us from an ancient Celtic Fire Festival, Beltane is a celebration of life, love, and fertility. The sun has returned, and the land is blossoming. The god and the goddess are at the height of their youth and vigor, and they renew the earth with the consummation of their love.

Today, we come to this circle to rejoice in the light and the warmth, and the potential that this season brings. And we rejoice that we are here together! Let the revels begin!"

- HPS/HP start drumming. All in circle start drumming.

HPS/HP:

We drum the heartbeat of the earth. We drum the pulse of life. We drum the rhythm of love. We drum because we are Witches and all these things are a part of who and what we are.

- Drumming

And as we drum, we touch the gods, and the gods touch us. And in this union, we can feel our own power, and our own potential.

- One at a time, as you are moved to do so, pick a ribbon from the altar, and tie it around the May bush (a bush or pole should be clearly indicated in some way before the ritual starts—a large ribbon or a star will do.) Each ribbon signifies a wish for the year to come—you may speak yours aloud, or say it silently.
- The drumming continues, and participants place ribbons on the bush or pole one by one. It's fine for people to do so more than once. People can also dance around the circle if they are so moved. When everyone has finished, including the HPS and/or HP, the drumming stops.

HPS/HP:

"From times long passed, people have jumped the Beltane fires to bring good luck and prosperity in the year ahead. Who will be the first to leap the fires today?"

- One by one, participants can jump over either the bonfire—if it is small—or a small fire or candle placed in a cauldron instead. Couples may jump the fire together if they want to. Everyone else should clap and cheer as each person jumps.

HPS/HP: [Holds up chalice]

We celebrate the fertility of the land, and vow to do our part to nurture the earth our Mother. [Pours mead or juice from the chalice onto the ground.] We pour a libation to the god and goddess. [Pour again.] We pour a libation to the fairies that rule unseen. [Pour again.] We pour a libation to love!

- Pass the chalice around the circle for cakes and ale. Each person in the circle says, "May you give and receive love with an open heart."
- Pass cakes "May your life be sweet."
- Pass the speaking stick.
- Dismiss the quarters.

HP thanks the god:

Great God, we thank you for your presence in our circle and in our lives. May you shine your bright light on us always. Farewell and blessed be.

HPS thanks the goddess:

Great Goddess, we thank you for your presence in our circle and in our lives. May you share your love with us always. Farewell and blessed be.

- Open the circle by reciting the Wiccan Rede:

Bide the Wiccan Law ye must

In perfect love and perfect trust

Eight words the Wiccan Rede fulfill

An it harm none, do as ye will

Lest in thy self defense it be

Ever mind the law of three

Follow this with mind and heart

And merrie ye meet and merrie ye part!

The circle is open, but never broken.

• • •

- Feast!

May New Moon

Love charm sachet

The theme for the month of May is love. For the New Moon, we often craft magickal objects or tools to be used in later magickal workings. This month, your group can make a love charm sachet to use during the Full Moon ritual in a couple of weeks—or any time you need it.

Sachets or charms are usually created by taking a bag or piece of cloth and filling it with herbs, gemstones, or other objects that contain magickal potential. The bag is then closed, or tied with ribbon, and consecrated. Sometimes a spell is said over the charm, to give it even more power.

Charm bags may be made out of plain muslin, or you can use silk or cotton cloth (always use a natural material.) If you want, you can use a color that is associated with the type of magick you are doing. For love, it should be white or pink. The one used for prosperity work should be green.

Remember that as you craft your charm or sachet, you should be focusing all your intent on the goal you wish to achieve. It is this that makes the charm work, not just the herbs you put inside.

supplies:

❑ A pink, white, or red bag or piece of cloth

❑ If using cloth, a pink, gold, or white ribbon to tie it with

❑ The following herbs: rosebuds or petals, lavender, rosemary, carnation, cinnamon, marigold (calendula). You do not have to use all of these, although you can. Try to have at least four of the six listed. The flowers can be fresh or dried, the cinnamon should be in stick form, and not powdered, if possible.

• • •

- Consecrate and cleanse the circle by passing sage or incense (if using incense, try lavender or rose.)
- Consecrate and cleanse the circle by passing salt and water.
- Cast the circle.
- Call the quarters.

HPS invokes the goddess:

Great Goddess, from whom all love flows, help us in our magickal work tonight. Welcome, and blessed be.

- Sit in circle and make yourselves comfortable. (This is a good time to use quiet background music.) Each of you should take a bag or piece of cloth on which to place your herbs. Pass the herbs around the circle (it is nice to use decorative ritual bowls, but not necessary.) As the herbs are passed, the HPS should say out loud why that particular plant is being used:
  › *Rosebuds or petals* to find or keep love
  › *Lavender* to attract love
  › *Rosemary* for love, lust, and memory
  › *Carnation* to add spice to love
  › *Cinnamon* for passion
  › *Marigold* for strength, and to comfort the heart

As each herb is placed in the cloth, concentrate on its gift, and how you wish to use it. When the bags are filled, close them, or tie them with ribbon, and take a moment of silence to focus your will and intent. Then say the spell together, repeating it three times (three is a magickal number, and repeating spells increases their power):

Love as a blessing

Love without harm

Love filled with sweetness

I call with this charm.

If you like, you can even write the spell on a piece of paper and slip it into the bag.

Later, you can hang the charm by your altar, place it under your pillow, or carry it with you as needed.

- Pass cakes and ale.
- Pass the speaking stick.
- Dismiss the quarters.

HPS thanks the goddess:

Great Goddess, help us find the love we seek, and keep the love we have. We thank you for the love in this circle tonight, and for the love you bring us always. Farewell and blessed be.

- Open the circle.

May Full Moon

Opening to love ritual

Love spells are one of the hardest kinds of magick to get right. For every Witch who will tell you that she met her true love after casting a love spell, there are three more with terrible—although often funny— stories about how a love spell brought only disaster. I've got a couple of those stories myself, so I know whereof I speak. Oh, fine—go ahead and laugh.

They are also hard to write without breaking any of the rules. Remember that in Wicca you should never do anything that interferes with someone else's free will. And since a love spell usually involves someone besides yourself (at least in theory), you must take extra care not to write or cast a spell that forces someone to love you. It's not nice, it's not fair . . . and it will get your butt kicked by the karma police. *Just don't do it.*

Even if you know exactly who you want to have love you, these spells are hard to write. They're even tougher if you haven't met the right one yet, and want a spell to call him or her into your life. Even worse is when you are in a relationship that is failing, and you want to cast a spell to make your partner stay. Repeat after me: free will, free will, free will.

Beware of fooling yourself into thinking that you are doing something for someone else's good. For example, "He'll be happier if I make him love me," or "I know the gods intended her to be with me; she just hasn't figured it out yet."

I know a Witch who cast a spell to bring back the man she was sure that she wanted. Unfortunately, when she finally realized that they had broken up that first time for a reason, she found out that her spell had bound him to her so strongly that she couldn't get rid of him. They split up, only to get back together again, and even after the final breakup, he stalked her on and off for years. The lesson here is the oft-repeated saying, *Be careful what you wish for. You just might get it.*

The moral of this story is simple. If you decide to use a love spell, be very, very careful. It is a lot trickier than it seems.

So what's a lonely Witch to do? Well, you could try doing a spell that doesn't involve anyone other than yourself.

Sometimes, without being aware of it, we put up barriers to love. Even when we know we're doing it, this can be a hard thing to fix. People put up walls to keep themselves from being hurt, and then they don't know how to take them down again. Couples grow apart and can't seem to find their way back to each other, no matter how hard they try. Or maybe they just stop trying.

The May Full Moon ritual in this chapter contains a possible remedy for all these problems, and can be useful in dealing not just with romantic love, but also the love between family, friends, and more. Rather than being a spell to find love, or keep love, it is simply a spell to be open to love.

When casting this spell, the intention is to remove those barriers that we—purposely or without knowing—put up to keep love out. If we are open to love, in all its forms, then maybe that perfect mate will finally see us, a partner will feel safe to open up to love again, or a family rift will start to mend. As with all magick, there are no guarantees. Much depends on your will and your intent. But unlike most love spells, this one is much less likely to backfire on you.

Yes, it is always a risk to let love in. But Wicca is all about taking those risks, in search of the greater good. It is said in Wicca: love is the law, and love is the bond. At its very core, love is what Wicca is all about, the essence of being a Witch. May you find the love you seek, and may it warm your heart and gladden your spirit. *So mote it be.*

suppLies:

❑ The love charm that you made at New Moon (if you didn't make charms for some reason, and don't want to make them, you can buy love sachets from catalogs, or buy them online or at a local Wiccan store if you're lucky enough to have one nearby.)

❑ Pink candles (one for each of you, and a big one to use as the goddess candle or a group candle if you wish.)

❑ Anointing oil (rose is traditionally used for love spells, but real rose essential oil can be expensive, so you can also substitute lavender, gardenia, or another flower blossom oil.)

❑ Optional: a piece of rose quartz (one for each group member is best, but share if you have only one.)

❑ Optional: rose incense (if no one is allergic. Otherwise, lavender or some other natural scent is fine.)

• • •

- Consecrate and cleanse the circle with rose or lavender incense.
- Consecrate and cleanse the circle with salt and water.
- Cast the circle.
- Call the quarters.

HPS invokes the goddess:

Great Goddess, we gather under the Full Moon to work our Craft in your name, and with your blessing. Help us to find love, and keep love, to give love and accept love, in any way that is positive and beneficial. For you have taught us, and we know that it is true—love is the law and love is the bond. So mote it be. (Light a pink goddess candle if you are using one.)

Sit comfortably and talk for a few minutes about what love means to each of you. Discuss the ways in which love is already in your lives, and the ways in which you feel it is lacking. (Don't forget that love is not just about romance, but also about family, friendship, pets, and, of course, the love of your group and of the gods.) You may wish to figure out exactly how you want love to manifest—whether you want to, say, get along better with your family or meet the perfect man—and what things you can do to help make that happen.

Hold, or place in your lap, the love charm you made at New Moon, and the piece of rose quartz. (If you have only one, you can leave it on the altar.) Hold your pink candle in your other hand and visualize your heart and spirit opening up. Close your eyes if that makes visualizing easier for you. See yourself welcoming in love in all its positive and beneficial forms, surrounded with a glow of love and of happiness. If you are trying to be open to a particular kind of love, such as romantic love, visualize yourself in the situation that you are hoping to bring about. (If you are having family issues, for instance, you can see everyone sitting around the dinner table laughing and talking.) Pass the oil around the circle, and anoint your candle with it, while focusing on being open to love.

When everyone is ready, say this spell together:

open to Love spell

I call upon the goddess wise

To open heart, and mind and eyes

To see potential where it lies

I call upon the goddess wise

I call upon the goddess strong

To send me love for which I long

To help me sing a loving song

I call upon the goddess strong

I call upon the goddess fair

To help me love and help me care

To give me courage, help me dare

I call upon the goddess fair

I call upon the goddess wise

To open heart and mind and eyes

To see her love in every guise

I call upon the goddess wise

In this I swear I'll do my part

To open up a loving heart

So mote it be

• • •

Have a moment of silence. (Note that you can burn your candle immediately, later that evening, or whenever you feel the need. You can use this spell as often as you feel you need it, replacing the candles as they burn down. Love magick is usually done on Fridays, but this type of spell can be done on any day or every day, as necessary.)

- Take a deep breath and ground, letting go of the intense energy and feelings that may have arisen during the spell casting. (After all, love is emotional and powerful.)
- Pass cakes and ale (this is a good time for chocolate anything!)
- Pass the speaking stick.
- Dismiss the quarters.

HPS thanks the goddess:

Great Goddess, beautiful and wise, we thank you for the love we share with each other and with you. Although the moon may wax and wane, your love is a constant, on which we can depend. For love is the law, and love is the bond. Thank you for your presence in our circle and in our lives. Farewell, and blessed be.

- Open the circle.

✿ Notes

_____   _____
_____   _____
_____   _____
_____   _____
_____   _____
_____   _____
_____   _____
_____   _____
_____   _____
_____   _____
_____   _____
_____   _____
_____   _____
_____   _____
_____   _____
_____   _____
_____   _____
_____   _____

juNe

...ner Solstice, also known as Midsummer, or Litha. The solstice falls on ...Check a calendar for the exact date.)

...day of the year, and we revel in the abundance of light and growth. ...hen the earth is at its most fertile and full of life, as a representation of ...t of their powers. The goddess, as Mother, is pregnant with the child ...d the whole world is blossoming.

...handfastings (pagan wedding rituals) and celebrations of family life.

If at all possible, the Summer Solstice should be celebrated outside, with heaps of flowers on the altar. You may want to welcome children into the circle, even if you do not normally do so, and invite the significant others of your group members to attend if they would like to get a taste of what Wicca is all about in a non-threatening atmosphere. (Remember to go over the basics of ritual etiquette with anyone who has never come to a circle gathering before, and remind parents to keep an eye on their children.)

Midsummer ritual

suppLies:

❏ Bowl full of dried lavender

❏ Small muslin bags (or small cloth bundles) filled with edible seeds like pumpkin and sunflower.

Note: If you cannot do this ritual outside around a small bonfire, you can substitute a cauldron or large bowl filled with candles, and use only a small amount of lavender instead of a handful.

• • •

- All enter the circle.
- Consecrate and cleanse the circle by passing sage—or have someone walk around the outside of the circle with sage or incense. (You may want to use a large feather to waft the smoke toward people.)
- Consecrate and cleanse the circle by passing salt and water—or have one circle member walk around sprinkling salt, then another follow sprinkling water.
- Cast the circle by having the High Priestess or High Priest walk around the outside of the circle with an athame or sword pointing at the ground. (See chapter 17 for words to say if so desired.)
- Call the quarters.

HPS invokes the goddess:

I call the Great Goddess, she who is Mother of us all, who brings us the green bounty of the land, and gift of family and friends. Join us in our circle as we celebrate this holiday in your honor!

HP invokes the god:

I call the Great God, he who is Lord of the Sun, who brings us the gifts of light and energy. Join us now in our circle as we celebrate this holiday in your honor!

HPS/HP:

We have gathered here in this sacred space to celebrate the Summer Solstice, also known as Midsummer, or Litha. The Solstice marks the longest day of the year and the shortest night. The goddess is in her aspect of Mother, pregnant and abundant, and her consort, the god, is at the height of his power. The earth itself is at its most fertile, and we prepare ourselves for the harvest to come, gathering up light and energy while they are available to us.

On the Solstice, we bid farewell to the waxing half of the year, domain of the Oak King, and welcome in the waning half of the year, ruled by his brother the Holly King. We revel in the sunlight, and honor the goddess and god by bringing forth our own passions as they have brought forth theirs.

HPS/HP:

I will now lead us in a meditation to help us get in touch with the energy of Earth and Sun that are so abundant at this time of year. Please sit, and make yourselves as comfortable as possible. (Read slowly and calmly.)

Close your eyes. Take a slow, deep breath. Now, another. Feel the strength of the earth underneath you. Solid and dependable, that strength is always there for you to call on if you need it. In your mind's eye, see yourself putting roots down into the ground. Coming out of your tailbone, growing ever deeper, feel them reaching down into the earth and connecting with that strength, that energy for growth. Feel that energy climbing up from the earth, and filling you with strength and calm and focus.

Now, reach upward and feel the power and clarity that comes from above. Breathe it in to the deepest core of your being. Feel the energy of the sun as it races through your veins, and recharges your physical, mental, and spiritual batteries. Feel the light washing away all your stresses and cares, leaving only strength and calm and focus.

You are one with the earth. You are one with the sky. You are at peace.

Take a few slow, deep breaths, and fill yourself with as much of that light and energy and strength as you can hold. Then, when you are ready, open your eyes, and be ready to bring all of your focus and intent to the next part of our ritual.

HPS/HP:

It is traditional for Witches to throw the herb lavender into the midsummer bonfire, as a sacrifice to the gods. Since this is a day to prepare ourselves to be at our most productive, it is also a good time to let go of those things that stand in the way of us achieving our goals. We will pass around a bowl of lavender. When it reaches you, grab a handful and throw it into the fire, and declare your intention to sacrifice whatever you feel interferes with your own power and energy. This can be anything from illness to debt, self-doubt to a soul-sapping job. Whatever it is, focus all your will on sacrificing this part of your life, which stands in the way of growth and productivity. Then throw it into the fire along with the herb, and hand the bowl to the next person. The bowl can travel around the circle until everyone is done.

- The bowl is passed around the circle. Make sure you have enough lavender for it to go around several times if necessary.

HPS/HP:

At Midsummer, the goddess is overflowing with growth—joyful in her role as pregnant Mother, and carrying within her all the hope and potential for the year to come. As we have created this sacred space to celebrate in her name, so we ask her to join us now, and share with us her gifts for potential and growth.

HPS:

Great Goddess, we call you now!

- A circle member steps forward and says loudly, "I am here!" This person is representing the goddess—so she should dress accordingly and speak with dignity as she goes around the circle saying to each participant, "I give you these bundles of pumpkin and sunflower seeds. May they sustain your body and spirit, and hold the seeds for all you desire." (She gives out bundles of edible seeds to everyone in circle.)

HPS:

We will now drum and chant to raise energy. Draw that energy into your packet of seeds, so that when you eat them later you can take the goddess's gift within yourself, and use it for whatever you need.

- Drumming and chanting to raise energy. (You can use the chant that goes: "Fire am I, Water am I, Earth and Air and Spirit am I" if you know it. See chapter 17 for more chants.)

- Ground and center.

- Pass cakes and ale. (This is a good mead holiday.)

- Pass the speaking stick.

- Dismiss the quarters.

- HPS thanks the goddess.

- HP thanks the god.

- Open the circle.

- Have a feast if you like!

June New Moon

Family healing spell

June is a great time to celebrate family, whether it is the family you are born with or the family you choose, such as your circle or coven. Unfortunately, we don't all have great relationships with our families, and even the best groups occasionally have problems.

At one point during the year, it seemed as if almost everyone in Blue Moon Circle was having issues with a parent, a sibling, or both (although, thankfully, we weren't having any problems with each other!) So, we cast this spell to help us heal the wounds and close the gaps. Remember that, as with all spells, you have to take suitable action as well—even if that action is nothing more than trying to keep an open mind and a loving heart.

This spell can be done any time that some or all of the group members need it, and it can be done by an individual as easily as by a group.

- Cleanse and consecrate the circle with sage or incense.
- Pass water and salt around the circle.
- If you made peace and happiness oil, have each member anoint the person next to her or him (or you can substitute any other oil that is appropriate).
- At the third eye—located between the eyes—say "May you always see clearly."
- Near the mouth—say "May you always speak the truth with compassion."
- Over the heart—say "May you give and receive love freely."
- Cast the circle hand to hand.
- Call the quarters.

HPS invokes the goddess:

Great Goddess, you who are Mother of us all, we your children greet you and beseech you to join us in our sacred circle. Aid us in our search for clarity, compassion, and peace, and help us in our work here tonight. Blessed be.

Talk a little bit around the circle about whatever problems people are having with their families. Try not to be overly negative or judgmental—just discuss the problems, and the impact they are having on each circle member's life. If someone gets emotional, that's fine. But don't spend too much time talking about any one person's issues. You may want to all state out loud the intention to make changes for the better in your family situation. If the problems are in your "circle family," try to discuss them calmly, without pointing fingers or accusing anyone. It is helpful to say, "This situation makes me feel" rather that "You make me feel," so that no one gets the sense that they are under attack. Try to see things from the other person's point of view.

Once you have talked about the problems, put your attention on the goddess candle in the middle of your circle or altar table. Focus on your intention to heal the wounds and resolve the problems. Feel yourself filling with love. If you are not in a particularly loving frame of mind, ask the goddess to help you—she always has plenty of love to spare. Whoever is leading the ritual might say the following out loud:

"Goddess, we ask you to fill our hearts with love and our spirits with compassion."

When everyone is focused, recite the spell together:

family healing spell

Children of the goddess are we

Central to our family tree

Maiden, Mother, Crone, and all

On this night, to you we call

Bless the families from which we spring

Ease the tortured hearts that sting

Aid Forgiveness, ease all pain

Make the broken whole again

Help us see the hearts of others

Children, siblings, and our mothers

Forgiveness grant to those in need

And reward the selfless deed

Heal the bonds that family bind

Heal the heart, the soul, the mind

Bring peace to troubled hearts at last

With this spell by Witches cast

So mote it be

• • •

If you are in an all-woman group, you can substitute the word "daughters" for "children" in the first line, and "sisters" for "Witches" in the last line, if you like.

After a moment of silence, go around the circle and each take a turn telling of something you can do to make your situation better. This is very important, as you need to use the power of the spell to help you find practical solutions (and it will).

- Pass cakes and ale.
- Pass the speaking stick.
- Dismiss the quarters.
- HPS thanks the goddess.
- Open the circle. This is a good time to recite the Wiccan Rede.

June Full Moon

Protection spell

The world we live in can be a frightening and uncertain place. It is hard not to feel vulnerable when faced with the possibilities of natural disasters, household accidents, and people with bad intentions. We all do whatever we can to protect ourselves and those we love, but there are times when none of the precautions we take seem like enough.

Fortunately, as Witches, we know that we can do just a little bit more. The protection spell in this chapter is designed for house (or apartment) protection, but it can be used for your car, a specific room, or even a particular person, as needed.

As with most of the spells in this book, you can use this one whenever you feel the need, and an individual can do it as easily as a group can do it. If you are trying to protect a space, it is a good idea to renew the spell once a year. For example, I have gone around the outside of my house and the boundaries of my property on a regular basis since I moved here.

supplies:

❑ Dried or fresh rosemary and basil

❑ Sea salt

❑ Rosemary essential oil

❑ White candle

❑ Squares of white cloth (silk or cotton)

❑ Red yarn

❑ Pins

❑ Garlic cloves

❑ Some tumbled agate stones or beads

Notes: You can get herbs and essential oils from local pagan or health-food stores, or there are many sources for ritual supplies online. Of course, the best herbs for magickal use are always those you have grown yourself.

When using salt for cleansing or protection purposes in a ritual, sea salt is usually considered to be best. Many pagan and New Age stores sell tumbled semi-precious gemstones, but if you don't have agates, you can just look for an interesting small rock that appeals to you or use agate beads if you have them.

·   ·   ·

- If you want, before the ritual you can scatter rosemary, basil, and salt around the area you wish to be protected.
- Cleanse and consecrate the circle by passing sage. (This is one time when you should use sage instead of incense, if you have it.)
- Cleanse and consecrate the circle with water and salt.
- Cast the circle.
- Anoint the quarter candles with rosemary oil. Call the quarters.
- HPS anoints the white goddess candle with rosemary oil. Invoke the goddess: "Hestia, goddess of the hearth, you have protected homes and hearts since time out of mind. Attend us now, and aid us in our protection rite. Welcome, and blessed be."

HPS:

"In order to enjoy our lives, we must feel safe. Tonight we will create charms of protection, which will render our homes as safe as our circles."

- Take a square of white cloth. While you concentrate on feelings of safety and protection, place in your cloth a few pins, a pinch or two of rosemary and basil, a clove of garlic, and some salt. Chose a stone that feels right, and place it in the center of your cloth. Tie up your charm with a piece of red yarn and consecrate it with a few drops of rosemary oil.

- When everyone is ready, hold your charm bundle up above the altar and say:

  I make this charm, full of power

  To guard my home from this hour.

- (If you want to repeat the spell when placing the charm in your home, you should say, "I place this charm full of power, to guard my home from this hour.")

HPS:

I call upon Hestia to bless these charms, created in her name. I call upon her to bless this house, and the land it sits upon, and all that reside within it. Protect all those here from harm from within or without, accidental or intentional. Bring in all that is positive and drive out all that is negative. Watch over us always. So mote it be.

If creating a charm for something other than your home, substitute the appropriate words, such as: "I call upon her to bless this car, that it may carry me in safety" or "I call upon her to bless the woman, that she may always walk in safety."

- Pass cakes and ale.
- Pass the speaking stick.
- Dismiss the quarters.

HPS thanks the goddess

Great Hestia, we thank you for your presence in our circle, and for your help with our magickal working tonight. May you continue to watch over us in the days to come, and lend us your protection wherever we go. Thank you, and blessed be.

- Open the circle.

@ Notes

_____   _____
_____   _____
_____   _____
_____   _____
_____   _____
_____   _____
_____   _____
_____   _____
_____   _____
_____   _____
_____   _____
_____   _____
_____   _____
_____   _____
_____   _____
_____   _____

juLy

For many of us, July is one of the busiest months of the year. Although the summer is theoretically a time for vacations, recreation, and rest, the reality is that most of us are more active than ever. Whether we are dealing with our yard and garden, kids out of school, or just trying to fit that vacation into our hectic schedules, we often find ourselves trying to keep even more balls in the air than usual.

For Blue Moon Circle, July was a time when we all felt that because there was so much to do, we ended up not accomplishing anything. As I talked to the various members of the group, I noticed that we all felt the same way; we were being pulled in too many directions and couldn't focus on any one thing enough to actually complete it successfully. We were all frustrated and overwhelmed. What's a Witch to do?

To address the problem I came up with a spell. Two spells, in fact. And a charm. (What can I say? It was a *big* problem.) The end result was the focus and achievement spells that you will find in this chapter.

Start Part One of the spell in circle at the New Moon, and repeat it individually every night—or as many nights as you can manage—during the waxing moon. Start Part Two of the spell together at the Full Moon, and repeat that individually as often as possible during the waning moon.

As with all the other spells in this book, feel free to use these any time you feel the need. You can hang the charm bag by your altar or at work, or carry it with you.

The focus and achievement spells turned out to be among Blue Moon's most powerful and effective magickal workings. I hope they work as well for you.

July New Moon

Focus and achievement spell—part one: waxing moon

supplies:

- ❏ White or green bags, or pieces of cloth (one for each person)
- ❏ Dried or fresh herbs: chamomile, lavender, rosemary, carnation, cinnamon
- ❏ Hematite (tumbled stones are best, but beads or chips will work if that is all you can find.)
- ❏ String or ribbon to tie the bags.

When making charms or sachets, the best herbs to use are those you have grown yourself. If you don't have a garden, you might try growing a few magickal herbs on a windowsill—you will be surprised by how easy, and how satisfying, it is to grow your own. If this isn't feasible, you can often get herbs at your local pagan store (if there is one), or health-food store.

When making this charm bag, I like to use dried chamomile and carnations (for ease of use), but fresh lavender and rosemary (because they smell so much stronger). I use pieces of cinnamon sticks, rather than powdered, but either will work.

Focus and achievement ritual

- Cleanse and consecrate the circle space by passing sage or incense. If people are feeling especially unfocused, you may want to give this part of the ritual even more attention than usual. It is a good idea to play calming music in the background, and burn a few extra candles for atmosphere. Do whatever it takes to help everyone get in the proper mental space for doing this work.

- Consecrate and cleanse the circle with salt and water.

- Cast the circle hand to hand.

- Call the quarters. You can ask for appropriate help from the elements. For instance: ask the element of Air to blow away confusion, the element of Fire to burn away stress, the element of Water to wash away clutter, and the element of Earth to ground you.

- HPS invokes the goddess.
- Once you are settled, you can put together your charm bags. You should have all the ingredients on your altar or table. Spread out your cloths (or open your bags) and place the herbs inside, one by one. Remember to be mindful of your intention as you work. To help you focus, you may want to list the parts of the charm one by one out loud as you add them.

Focus and achievement charm bag

- In a white or green bag or piece of cloth, combine:
    › Chamomile (for prosperity)
    › Lavender (for love and peace)
    › Rosemary (to strengthen mental powers)
    › Carnation (to instill strength)
    › Cinnamon (to attain success)
    › Add a piece of Hematite (for healing and grounding)

Tie the bag with string or ribbon and use with the focus and achievement spell.

When your charm bags are finished, take a moment of silence, then light a green or white candle, and recite the spell together.

focus and achievement ritual-part one

Goddess great, please shine your light

Bring more clarity to my sight

Help focus mind and heart and will

And with achievement hours fill

So I might rise above the rest

To do those things that I do best

Help me move with ease and grace

Through this life of frantic pace

Achieving more with every day

As I walk the blessed way

So mote it be

• • •

- Take a minute to enjoy your renewed energy and focus, then pass cakes and ale.
- Pass the speaking stick. This is a good time for people to talk about the things they want to focus on in the days to come.
- Dismiss the quarters.
- HPS thanks the goddess.
- Open the circle. Go home and start getting things done!

July Full Moon

Focus and achievement spell—part two: waning moon

This two-part spell is a perfect example of the difference between magick done during the waxing moon, and magick done during the waning moon. Remember that the waxing moon is used for **increase** and the waning moon is used for **decrease**.

So, for instance, if you were going to do magickal work for prosperity, you might do a spell to bring in more money during the waxing moon, and a spell to get rid of debt during the waning moon (while, of course, actively working in your mundane life to bring about both changes).

In this case, we did part one of the focus and achievement spell starting at the New Moon and then continuing through the two weeks of the waxing moon to increase focus and achievement, just as the name of the spell suggests. During the waning moon, however, this spell isn't as appropriate. So we will do part two starting at the Full Moon, and continuing through the two weeks of the waning moon. This part of the spell, rather than trying to increase focus, is designed to decrease stress and confusion. Same goal, two different approaches. I hope that both will get you where you want to be.

Note: If you are doing this spell during a year when the Full Moon in July falls before the New Moon, just reverse the order in which you do the spells.

Note: This is a very simple ritual. You can add more elements, but sometimes simple is better. This is another ritual where it is nice to have quiet spiritual music playing in the background.

- Cleanse and consecrate the circle by passing sage or incense.
- Cleanse and consecrate the circle by passing salt and water.
- If you wish, you can take turns anointing the group member next to you with the peace and happiness oil you created in February.
- If you have one, ring a bell or gong three times to focus yourselves and draw the attention of the gods to your magickal work.
- Cast the circle hand to hand.

- Call the quarters. (Again, you can ask their help with this task, as you did at New Moon, if you so desire.)
- HPS invokes the goddess.
- This would be a good time to have someone read *The Charge of the Goddess*. (If you don't have it, I suggest you look in a book, or go online—this is one of the most beautiful and moving pieces of Wiccan writing that there is.)
- If you want, you can talk about what happened after you did Part One of the spell at New Moon.
- Start drumming to build energy. Begin slowly and steadily, then increase in strength. Drum as long as people want to—maybe quite a while. When you feel that you have brought the level of energy in the circle to its peak, recite the spell together.

focus and achievement ritual—part two

Banish now this frantic pace

And bring me peace in sacred space

Wash away all stress and woe

And let my thoughts like rivers flow

Let confusion fade away

So I might focus on my day

Blow away the small distractions

That impede my will and actions

All those things that cloud my focus

Vanish now with "hocus pocus"!

(It's fun to yell out that last bit together—try it and see!)

• • •

- When you have stopped laughing and have caught your breath, pass cakes and ale. This is a nice time to have something a little self-indulgent . . . chocolate cake maybe?
- Pass the speaking stick. If you didn't do it in the beginning, this is a good time to compare notes on what effect the first part of the spell had on everyone.
- Dismiss the quarters.
- HPS thanks the goddess.
- Open the circle.

❂ Notes

_____   _____
_____   _____
_____   _____
_____   _____
_____   _____
_____   _____
_____   _____
_____   _____
_____   _____
_____   _____
_____   _____
_____   _____
_____   _____
_____   _____
_____   _____
_____   _____
_____   _____

august

The month of August starts out with Lammas, the first of the three Wiccan harvest festivals. Lammas falls on August first, and is also known as Lughnasadh—in honor of Lugh, the Celtic god of light. Lammas is a celebration of grain, and of the successful beginning of the summer harvest season. Since early Pagans depended on the land for their lives, many of the holidays we celebrate today have their roots in the interconnectedness between the land, the people, and the gods who ensured their continued survival.

These days, we can go to the grocery store to buy our bread, and not every Witch has a garden full of herbs and vegetables (although it is strongly recommended . . .). But that doesn't mean that we can't celebrate the season, and celebrate whatever it is that is coming to fruition in our lives.

After all, there is more than one type of harvest. At Lammas, we also celebrate our mental, physical, and spiritual bounty. Throughout the year, we have worked toward growth, and for various goals in our lives. Lammas is the time to check in on our progress, and to reap the rewards of our hard work, both magickal and mundane.

Lammas ritual

- Use a ritual broom (if you have one) to sweep around the circle.
- Consecrate and cleanse the circle with sage.
- Consecrate and cleanse the circle with salt and water.
- Cast the circle hand to hand.
- Call the quarters.

High Priestess invokes the goddess:

I invoke the Goddess Demeter—lady of the grain, goddess of the harvest, bountiful Mother who provides us with food for our tables and nourishment for our souls. Be with us now as we honor you with this ritual and celebrate your gifts. Welcome, and blessed be.

High Priest invokes the god:

I invoke the God Lugh—lord of the fields, god of the sun, bringer of light, warmth, and abundance. Be with us now as we honor you with this ritual and celebrate your gifts. Welcome, and blessed be.

HPS/HP:

We come together today to celebrate Lammas, also known as Lughnasadh (Lew-nah-sah). Lammas is the first harvest festival, when bread is made from the newly ripe grains—a physical manifestation of the transformation of the sun's energy into sustenance for our bodies.

Circle member:

This is a time of rejoicing and a time of sorrow. We gather in this sacred space to honor the Corn King, god of the ripening fields, lord of the grain. We pledge our gratitude for the sacrifice he makes so that we may partake of nature's bounty, survive, and grow strong.

Circle member:

This is a time of hope, a time to gather strength against the coming darkness. We join together to turn the Wheel, knowing that to harvest we must also sacrifice, and that warmth and light must pass into winter. We know, too, that as long as we stand together, there will always be light in the darkness.

Circle member:

We trust in each other, and in the love of the god and goddess, and thus we know that we will grow and thrive throughout the year to come. We celebrate the harvest together, and rejoice at the bounty of our lives.

HPS:

This is also a time for spiritual harvest. Through the year, we have worked toward growth—tending the gardens of our lives with hard work, dreams, and magick. Now we reap the rewards of our labor, as we harvest strength, peace, prosperity, health, and love. And we know in our deepest hearts that all our dreams are possible.

Start drumming—and drum until you feel that the circle is full of energy. Then recite the Lammas spell together:

Lammas harvest spell

We have tilled the soil

And planted the seed

Long did we toil

To get what we need

The days now grow short

The wheel it has turned

We sowed root and wort

Now we reap what we've earned

We harvest our fields

Full of health, luck, and love

We gather great yields

Of our gifts from above

Prosperity grows

Even as the sun wanes

Happiness glows

Through the late summer rains

Our thanks overflowing

Our hearts filled with glee

We harvest our sowing

Shouting "So mote it be"!

• • •

- Ground.
- Pass cakes and ale. This is a good time to pass a round loaf of bread, and have everyone tear off a piece. Use either mead or juice in the chalice.
- Pass the speaking stick. (People can talk about what they hope to harvest, or what they have learned during the growing time.)
- Dismiss the quarters.
- HPS/HP thank the god and goddess:

HP:

Great god Lugh (Lew), we thank you for bringing your light to this circle, and to our lives. May you continue to shine down upon us until we meet again. Farewell, and blessed be.

HPS:

Great Goddess Demeter, we thank you for the bounty of the harvest, and for the bounty you have brought to our lives. Know that we are always grateful for the gifts that you bring. Farewell, and blessed be.

- Open the circle.
- *Feast!*

August New Moon

Adjusting to change spell

As you reap the harvest of your magickal work (not to mention the alterations that you have made in your everyday life), you will see many benefits. You may be stronger, wiser, more prosperous, healthier . . . thinner. Whatever you have been working on, you should be seeing some of the results by now. That's good, right? Of course it is.

Still, most people find change to be at least a bit unsettling, even if the change is for the better. Some of us get downright stressed out by the new and different, even if that is what we asked for in the first place. Here is a spell to help ease you through the transition to the new and improved you.

You can also use this spell any time you need help with some type of change, including the not-so-positive ones that life occasionally throws at us. It doesn't need to be done at one of the Moons to be effective, either. Just put all your need for help into it—and the goddess will hear you, no matter what the date.

This ritual is best done in a quiet atmosphere. If you like to play music in the background as you get started, turn it off before you call the quarters.

• • •

- Cleanse and consecrate the circle with sage or incense.
- Cleanse and consecrate the circle with salt and water.
- If desired, pass the peace and happiness oil (from February) around the circle. Have circle members anoint themselves while concentrating on becoming more at peace.
- Cast the circle, either hand to hand or by having the HPS walk around the circle with her athame.
- Call the quarters.

HPS invokes the goddess:

Great Goddess, Lady of the Moon, we welcome you. As the moon rules over the changes in the tides and in our bodies, so you rule over the changes in our spirits. We ask that you join us tonight, and aid us as we seek to deal with those changes with grace and dignity. So mote it be.

- Drum to raise energy. If your group likes to chant, this is a good time to do the "She changes everything She touches, and everything She touches changes" chant. Remember to focus on what you want to achieve with this magickal work.

- When you have raised the energy in the circle to its peak, recite the spell together. If some or all of the people in your group are in crisis, repeat the spell three times for added power.

adjusting to change spell

In time of change, to ease transition

I call upon the goddess wise

To help me find my new position

Underneath her moonlit skies

Guide my spirit, hands, and heart

In this time of shifting tide

Aid me with the tasks I start

While easing what I lay aside

Whether grief or joyous birth

Sadness or release

With Air and Water, Fire and Earth

The goddess brings me peace

So mote it be

. . .

- Take a moment of silence to ground, and let your new balance settle in.
- Pass cakes and ale. Comfort foods like cookies are good for this ritual.
- Pass the speaking stick.
- Dismiss the quarters.
- HPS thanks the goddess.
- Open the circle. (This is a good time to recite the Wiccan Rede.)

August Full Moon

Prosperity

The August Full Moon is the perfect time to do prosperity work. At the height of the summer, abundance is all around you. The Full Moon is a powerful night, and when you combine the two, any magickal work you do is almost sure to succeed.

Prosperity work is usually done on a Thursday night during the waxing moon (since you are working for increase). Does this mean that it won't work on a Wednesday during the waning moon? Of course not. As you know, intention and focus are the most important components of any magickal working. Nonetheless, many Witches think that the more "suitable" elements you can combine in any spell, the greater the likelihood of success. Certainly, more elements can't hurt. And as you put together those elements (candles, incense, and the rest), you are focusing more on your intentions. So it's all good.

The candle color used for prosperity work is green. Various incenses and oils that are appropriate include basil, bergamot, chamomile, cedar, cinnamon, clove, ginger, orange, peppermint, pine, and sage. If you don't have (or don't want to burn) incense, you can rub a drop or two of one of these essential oils onto the candle.

You may want to inscribe your candle with runes for added power (Blue Moon Circle almost always does so for this particular spell.) Use some or all of the following runes:

> *Gifu*—gifts and balance

> *Othel*—possessions, help, abundance

> *Ing*—success and relief

> *Fehu*—fulfillment, material gain, money

> *Sigel*—power, success

> *Uraz*—strength, will, change for the better

> *Jera*—rewards, fruitfulness

[See the Index of Runes on page 242]

You can also inscribe other symbols that have meaning to you, such as your initials, dollar signs, etc.

As always, remember that you can't just cast a spell and expect it to solve all your problems. You have to be actively pursuing solutions in your everyday life as well. For instance, if you need a new job, this spell can help to guide you to the right one—but only if you are out there looking for it.

I wrote this spell many years ago, and it has been used by me, members of both groups I've belonged to, and a number of spiritually inclined friends—often with amazing results. While it is theoretically most powerful when done on a Thursday or during the Full Moon, in times of need I have used it regardless of the day of the week or time of the month with good results. I hope it works as well for you.

SuppLies:

❏ Green candles. (You can use one for each person, or all make a group candle.)

❏ Incense or essential oil in an appropriate scent. (See the list above.)

❏ A paper with the runes for prosperity on it. (If you're going to use them.)

❏ Toothpicks, for carving the rune symbols.

•   •   •

• Cleanse and consecrate the circle with sage or incense.

• Cleanse and consecrate the circle with water and salt.

• Cast the circle, either hand to hand or by having the High Priestess walk around the outside of the circle with her athame or sword.

• Call the quarters.

• HPS invokes the goddess. Use the Full Moon invocation—see chapter 17.

• Each circle member should take his or her candle. If you are using an essential oil or a combination like your peace and happiness oil from February, rub a few drops on the candle. Work from the top down, moving around the candle clockwise. Be sure that the oil you are using will not cause sensitivity on contact with bare skin, as some oils are quite strong. Inscribe some or all of the runes for prosperity on the candle. You can use a toothpick or the tip of your athame. As you work, remember to concentrate on your intention of drawing prosperity into your life. If you want, you can inscribe your name or initials on the candle as well.

- When everyone is ready, read the spell together. Recite it three times, putting more energy and power into each recitation. By the end you may be shouting, which is fine.

onyx's prosperity spell

God and goddess hear my plea

Rain prosperity down on me

Bring in monies large and small

To pay my bills, one and all

Money earned and gifts for free

As I will, so mote it be

You may wish to add:

I cast this spell for the good of all,

And according to the free will of all, with harm to none

(After all, you don't want your prosperity to come because your favorite relative suddenly dies, leaving you everything.)

• • •

- Pass cakes and ale. Something rich and indulgent is called for here. When Blue Moon did this spell for the first time, we used fancy cookies and a decadent liqueur.
- Pass the speaking stick. This is a good time for each circle member to talk about what positive and practical measures they intend to take to increase prosperity in their lives.
- Dismiss the quarters.
- HPS thanks the goddess.
- Open the circle.

✪ Notes

_____   _____
_____   _____
_____   _____
_____   _____
_____   _____
_____   _____
_____   _____
_____   _____
_____   _____
_____   _____
_____   _____
_____   _____
_____   _____
_____   _____
_____   _____
_____   _____
_____   _____
_____   _____

CHAPTER 12

september

If you live in a part of the Northern Hemisphere with a distinct change of seasons, then you know that September brings with it the first signs of the winter to come. Although the days are still warm, the nights grow colder and the changing colors of the leaves warn us that the summer is drawing to a close.

On or about September twenty-first, we celebrate Mabon, the Autumn Equinox. As with the Spring Equinox, the light and dark are again in perfect balance. Now, though, we are moving away from the longer days of summer, and into the colder, darker, shorter days of winter. We let go of the hustle and bustle of the busy summertime, and start to prepare ourselves for the quieter hours of wintertime.

Mabon (*May-bon*) is the second of the three Wiccan harvest festivals. At this Equinox, we celebrate the fruits of our labors and the culmination of our magickal efforts in the proceeding year. We feast together on harvest foods like corn, squash, and apples, and we drink the sweet cider that reminds us of the sweetness in our lives. We give thanks to the gods for the many gifts they have bestowed upon us during the glorious sunlit days of summer.

Autumn Equinox/Mabon ritual

Note: If at all possible, this ritual should be done outside, around a small bonfire.

- Participants process into the circle to be greeted by HPS/HP, who hands out a spell for balance (found later in the ritual) and says, "Welcome, and blessed be."

- Once all are in circle, HPS/HP or circle member sweeps the circle with a broom and says, "We sweep this circle free of all negativity."

- Sage is lit and passed around the circle.

HPS/HP casts circle with athame (or sword):

> I draw this circle on the earth, a symbol of the yearly wheel
>
> The cycle of death and rebirth, to keep us safe, and help us heal
>
> We cast the circle round and round, making this a sacred place
>
> From the sky down to the ground, between all time between all space.

- Calling of the quarters:
- Circle member calls East: Light incense and say, "We summon the spirit of Air."
- Circle member calls South: Throw sage on fire and say, "We summon the spirit of Fire."
- Circle member calls West: Pour water on ground and say, "We summon the spirit of Water."
- Circle member calls North: Scatter salt on ground and say, "We summon the spirit of Earth."
- Invoking the gods:

HP:

> God of the Harvest
>
> Horned One of the Wilderness
>
> Bringer of bounty, healing and joy

We call you to attend our Rite

God of the Wines

God of the Fields

Be with us now in this circle out of time

And bless our work this night

HPS:

Blessed goddess

Autumn's Queen

Mother of all life

We call you to attend our Rite

Goddess of the Moon

Goddess of the Seas

Be with us now in this circle out of time

And bless our work this night

HPS/HP:

We come together tonight to celebrate the Autumn Equinox, also known as Mabon. This is the second harvest festival, the Witch's thanksgiving. At the equinox, day and night are equal, in perfect balance. And while this is a time of thanksgiving and joy, it is also a time of preparation for the coming darkness of winter. We can see the waning of the sun more clearly now, as the days continue to grow shorter until the Wheel of the Year spins around again to Yule. Spring and summer can often be times of tremendous growth and activity. At the Autumn Equinox, as we witness the balance of light and darkness in the world around us, so we reach for balance within ourselves. We take this moment for meditation and introspection, and ask that the gods help us to let go of the noise and confusion that often overwhelms our lives, making it difficult to appreciate our many blessings.

Tonight, in this sacred space, we have set the mundane world aside. Within this circle, there is only peace, and calm, and the love we share with the gods and with each other. Tonight, we will take that peace, and calm and love deep within, so that we may have it to sustain us during the quiet, darker days that lie ahead.

HPS/HP:

First, I will guide us through a short meditation, to quiet our bodies and spirits, and help us connect with the Mabon energies of balance and peace. Then, after a moment of silence, we will start to drum and clap to raise a cone of power within the circle. As you feel that power grow stronger, think of all those things in your life for which you are thankful, and feel yourself taking in balance and peace and joy with every breath. When the power is at its peak, I will give a signal, and we will stop drumming and recite the spell for balance together.

Read the "Meditation for Connecting with the Earth and Balancing the Soul" below. This meditation can be read by the HPS/HP or any circle member—people should make themselves comfortable:

Close your eyes. Take a few slow, deep breaths. Feel the quiet and calm within the circle start to sink into your soul. Breathe in the lingering smells of incense and sage. Listen to the sounds around you—sounds of birds, or insects, the sound of the person next to you breathing. Listen carefully, and you will hear a long slow sound, like the beat of a heart. Do you hear it? That is the sound of the earth our Mother, sitting beneath us. She breathes too. Can you feel it? Like a gentle massage, she surrounds us with her love, her strength, and her energy. Feel that energy sliding up your spine, into your heart, your mind, your spirit. Everywhere it touches, it leaves behind balance and peace, and a renewed connection to the earth from which we all come. Breathe deep and take in that energy, overflowing with love and compassion. Feel your heart fill with compassion for yourself and those around you. You are the earth, the breath, the peace that comes in this moment. You are whole and balanced, and ready to take that renewed sense of peace back out with you into your everyday life.

- Take a moment of silence.
- Drumming continues.
- Recite together: "Heart; Mind; Hands; Soul; Balanced; Open; Loving; Whole." (Recite multiple times.)

HPS/HP:

For the good of all, so mote it be.

- Pass the cakes and ale. Cider is perfect for this holiday, as is a loaf of homemade bread.

HPS/HP (cakes):

We give thanks for the grain that will sustain our bodies through the dark months to come, as our friendships sustain our spirit.

HPS/HP (ale):

We drink this cider, symbol of the season. May its sweetness remind us that the light always comes around again.

HPS/HP:

Now we pass the speaking stick—when it reaches you, feel free to share some of the things you gave thanks for, or say whatever is on your mind. Know that whatever is said within the circle, stays within the circle.

• Dismiss the quarters.

HP thanks the god:

God of the Harvest

We thank you for your sacrifice, freely made

So that Life may go on

And the Wheel continue in its circle

As it had been, so it will always be

We are grateful for all your gifts

And for your presence here tonight

Stay if you will, go if you must

In perfect love and perfect trust

So mote it be

HPS thanks the goddess:

Blessed goddess, Queen of the harvest

We thank you for the beauty of the season

And for your presence

In our lives, and at this ritual

Be with us through the coming cold and darkness

And help us to make the most of this quiet interlude

Before the new growth of spring

Stay if you will, go if you must

In perfect love and perfect trust

So mote it be

- Recite the Wiccan Rede if you like, and open the circle.
- Feast!

September New Moon

Herbal Magick ritual

September is the perfect time to practice herbal magick. The use of herbs for both magick and health goes back as far as written history, and probably beyond. The Witches of olden days were often the wise women of their villages, and they used herbs for everything from easing childbirth to creating love charms.

So, too, do we the Witches of the modern era call upon these powerful plants as tools to aid us in our Craft. Elsewhere in this book you will find plants used as parts of rituals, and as components of various spells and charms. They are as important a tool as your athame and your Book of Shadows . . . and many of them taste good, too.

September is the month when many herbs are ready to be harvested. They have spent the summer gathering power under the glow of the sun and the watchful eye of the moon. Now they are full of potent energy, ready to be used while they are fresh, or dried for use later on.

Remember that when you harvest herbs for magickal use that they should be treated with care and reverence, like the magickal tools they are. Never use your athame for cutting (it is strictly for symbolic use.) Some Witches keep a special curved knife called a *boline* especially for these types of tasks. Others just use a regular pair of scissors or clippers, but put particularly careful thought and intent into the act of cutting the plants.

Once the herbs are harvested, you can save them in special jars or containers, although there is nothing wrong with a plain old plastic bag, as long as it is airtight. You can bless and consecrate them as soon as they have been cut, or wait and do it later if you will not be using them immediately. Some Witches feel that if you have harvested your herbs with the proper reverence and intent, then they are consecrated by your very actions, and I tend to agree with this approach. However, it never hurts to say a few special words.

Some herbs are poisonous or dangerous if misused. A number of the traditional medicinal and magickal herbs that fall into this category can often be safely used for spells if they are not ingested. Nonetheless, I tend to stay away from these types of herbs, since so many safe ones are available and are just as effective. Be especially cautious if you have small children in the house.

The herbs that are found in this book are all mild, and many of them can be used for cooking and herbal medicine as well as for magick. In their essential oil forms, some of them can be irritating to the skin, and essential oils should usually not be taken internally. When doing herbal magick, essential oils can almost always be substituted for the fresh or dried forms of the herb, as long as you keep these points in mind.

The best herbs for magickal use are those that you have grown yourself and tended with care. If you live in a place where you cannot have a garden, many herbs can be grown inside—often with no more space than a windowsill. Even if you don't have room to grow all your magickal herbs yourself, having a few around will help you to keep in touch with nature, so I strongly recommend it.

This chapter contains information about a few of the herbs I use most often in magickal work and that I think your group will find the most useful. There are many wonderful books out there that go into much more depth on herbal magick than I have space for here, and I strongly suggest that you add at least a few of them to your magickal tool kit.

If you cannot grow your own herbs, you can usually find them at health food, New Age, and pagan shops, as well as many Wiccan sources online. Try to use herbs that are fresh and not treated with anything. (Most of the dried herbs found in the spice section of the grocery store are old, and many have been treated in one way or another.).

When my group did our New Moon herbal magickal work, we each chose three or four herbs to research, and we presented this research to the rest of the group. Doing so meant that we all got a lot of information without a lot of work on any one person's part—and it was fun to see what each person came up with, and what it revealed about his or her personality. Some group members even brought small pots with samples of the plants that they'd researched to give to the other members of the group.

We sat outside and passed the plants around, enjoying the smells and textures and the sharing of knowledge. All of us had a great time, and we got some cool plants to take home, too. I highly recommend that your group try this approach, if you can.

While it is fine for whoever is leading this ritual to do all the talking, it works very well if each group member takes a turn talking about a different herb. (See note above.)

suppLies:

❑ Fresh or dried herbs: including, if possible, lavender, chamomile, rosemary, and peppermint

• • •

- Cleanse and consecrate the circle with sage.
- Cleanse and consecrate the circle with salt and water.
- Cast the circle hand to hand or have the HPS walk around the circle with her athame.
- Call the quarters.

HPS invokes the goddess:

Great Goddess, lady of all that is green and growing, we call your name, and ask that you join us in our circle here tonight.

Take turns talking about various herbs. Research as many as your group is interested in, or use the following:

- Chamomile—also known as "ground apple." (part used: flowers)
  - › Magickal associations: planet = the sun; element = Water
  - › Powers: prosperity, meditation, calm
  - › Used in prosperity charms to draw money, helps bring on sleep, calm
  - › Used medicinally for calm and sleep, most often as an herbal tea.
- Lavender—also known as "elf leaf" (part used: flowers)
  - › Magickal associations: planet = mercury; element = Air
  - › Powers: love, protection, purification, peace, healing
  - › Used in baths, sachets, and incenses for purification, love, or healing. Rub on paper to be used for love letters. Carry it to see ghosts. Brings sleep, peacefulness. Traditionally thrown into the Midsummer fires by Witches as a sacrifice to the old gods.
  - › Used medicinally to help calm and induce sleep, and also to treat burns and infections.

- Rosemary—also known as "dew of the sea" (part used: leaves)
  › Magickal associations: planet = Sun; element = Fire
  › Powers: purification, love, protection, mind and intellect
  › Add to purification baths and sachets, love and protection incenses, exorcism mixes. Hang up to ward off thieves. Aids memory. Used in sea-related rituals. Make into an infusion (with hot water) and use to cleanse hands before working. Use in all protection sachets. (Blue Moon Circle puts a sprig or two into the water we use for circle cleansing and consecration.)
- Peppermint—also known as "brandy mint" (part used: leaves)
  › Magickal associations: planet=Venus or Mercury; element= Air or Fire
  › Powers: healing, purification, increase psychic powers
  › Add to healing incense and charms. Put a few drops of essential oil into a bath. Burn to cleanse the house during the winter. Use as a wash to purify the house. It has the bonus effect of getting rid of pests such as ants and mice.

Pass samples of herbs around the circle. Smell them. Touch them. If you have any favorite herbs, talk about them and tell the others in your group why you like them.

Have everyone take a sample of herb, and hold it up as you all recite together the following:

Goddess of the great unseen

Give to me your power green

Help me heal and help me know

With the fragrant herbs I grow

Doing good and never harm

With my herbal spell and charm

Like the Witch of olden days

Green and magick are my ways

So mote it be

• • •

- If you are using a bonfire or a small indoor cauldron, throw some dried herbs onto the fire at the end of the spell.

- Pass cakes and ale.

- Pass the speaking stick.

- Dismiss the quarters.

- HPS thanks the goddess.

- Open the circle.

September Full Moon

Healing Magick ritual — Creating magickal bath bags

Now that you have learned about some of the herbs used in magickal work, it is a good time to look at healing magick. Much of what Witches do has to do with healing—healing ourselves and healing others, and healing the physical, the emotional, the spiritual, and the psychic. On a higher level, you could even say that Wicca is about healing the earth, and the world as a whole.

That is a pretty big task, and for most of us, it is enough to try to help in some small way on a day-to-day basis. Many of the healing spells we employ call for the use of herbs in one way or another. Whether sewn into a sachet, burned as incense, or simply made up into a comforting tea, herbs are often an important part of healing work.

When using herbs, be sure to do your research. Do not eat or drink anything unless you are sure it is safe. *Never, **ever*** give an herbal remedy or potion to anyone without his or her knowledge. Not only does this go against the rule of free will, but also you never know when someone might be allergic to an otherwise safe herb. For instance, yarrow is a commonly used medicinal and magickal herb, which, sadly, makes me break out in blisters the size of large coins. I definitely would not want to drink it by accident.

supplies:

❑ Small muslin bags or "fill your own" tea bags (if you can't find muslin bags, you can make your own bags using the cheesecloth found in the cooking supplies section of most grocery stores)

❑ Dried or fresh peppermint, lemon balm, and lavender

❑ Sea salt and/or Epsom salts

❑ Dried oatmeal

❑ If you are making your own bags, white cotton thread

Note: These are called bath bags, but if you do not have a tub, they can also be used in the shower.

• • •

- Consecrate and cleanse the circle with sage or lavender incense.
- Consecrate and cleanse the circle with water and salt (if you want, you can add a drop of lavender essential oil.)
- Cast the circle hand to hand.
- Call the quarters.
- HPS invokes the goddess. (See the Full Moon invocation in chapter 17.)

HPS:

We work hard to keep ourselves healthy. As Witches, we know that all things are connected, and that eating unhealthy foods or surrounding ourselves with unhealthy people can only have a negative effect on our bodies, minds, and spirits. Yet the world is what it is. Some things are out of our control. And sometimes we are not as strong as we might wish to be.

So we come together tonight to renew our intention to take the steps that are necessary to control those things that we can, and to ask the goddess to help us with everything else.

Using the herbs that are her gift to us, we will create a magickal bath bag to aid us in this task.

- Take the herbs, the salt, and the oatmeal and put them together into your muslin bag or cloth. Focus on your intent to use this bag for healing, and on the healing properties of the materials you are using. You may want to think about the energy of the sun that went into growing the herbs, or—if you grew them yourself—the care that went into tending them. If you want, you can add a few drops of essential oil from one of the herbs you are using.
- When you have all put your bags together, close them up or tie them with thread, and recite the following spell together:

I am love and strength,

Energy and power

My health improves

With every hour

• • •

- Use the bag in a healing bath, or in the shower. Recite the spell again when you get into the water, and visualize the water washing away all that is negative and unhealthy.

- Pass cakes and ale.

- Pass the speaking stick. (This is a good time for everyone to say at least one thing that they plan to do to improve their health.)

- Dismiss the quarters.

- HPS thanks the goddess.

- Open the circle.

Notes

CHAPTER 13

OCTOBER

To most Witches, October means just one thing: Samhain! This holiday (pronounced *Sow-win*) is also known as the Witches' New Year, and falls on October thirty-first.

Most people know that date as Halloween, a spooky holiday characterized by ghosts and Witches. Halloween comes from the Christian holiday of All Hallows' Eve (Hallow Evening, or Hallow E'en), which in turn was adapted from the pagan celebration of Samhain.

As with most of the Christian holidays that were derived from pagan practices, the origins of Halloween's modern traditions can easily be traced back to its ancient pagan roots. The Witches . . . well, that one is obvious. (And for a change, everyone is dressing like us Witches, instead of the other way around!) The spookiness and the ghosts are descended from the pagan belief that on this day of the year, the veil between this world and the next is at its thinnest, allowing for communication between the living and the dead.

Samhain is the end of the Wiccan year. We take this opportunity to say goodbye to all those loved ones we have lost in the past year, and to speak to our ancestors if we have the need. At the same time, we celebrate the start of the new year with revelry and feasting. This may seem contradictory, but as Wiccans we know that sorrow and joy are both a part of life, and that neither can exist without the other.

Samhain is the third and final harvest festival, often featuring the apples, cider, pumpkins, and other squash that are so abundant at this time of year. It is also a time for divination. The holiday is represented by the colors of orange and black (the orange because of the fall colors, and the black for death, protection, and Witchcraft itself), and is usually celebrated at sundown, around a bonfire if at all possible.

This is the holiday that many Wiccans love the most—a time to rejoice with friends and fellow pagans, to let go of what has gone before and to celebrate what lies ahead. So dress up in your most Witchy black, grab your cloak and your broom, and revel in the joy of being a Witch!

Samhain—Triple goddess ritual

If you can manage it, this ritual should be performed outside, around a bonfire and at night. If it is absolutely impossible to be outside, you can substitute a cauldron or large bowl filled with candles for the fire. But Blue Moon Circle has done Samhain rituals in the cold, and in a drizzle, and it has always been worth the mild discomfort to be outside under the stars.

• • •

This ritual is quite different from the usual holiday rites, which tend to be lighthearted and fairly casual. This ritual is purposely designed to be very intense, and is an example of two Wiccan principles that are not always obvious in everyday practice.

The first important aspect of this ritual is that three women all act as High Priestess together. Despite the fact that most groups have one main High Priestess and/or High Priest, it is part of our beliefs that all Wiccans can act as priest or priestess. That practice is used here.

The second important aspect of this ritual is that the three women are representing the three forms of the goddess: Maiden, Mother, and Crone. There are times during ritual that the High Priest and/or High Priestess are considered to be actually channeling the gods through their words and actions. In this ritual, the three women speak as if they are the goddess incarnate—and, if done correctly, that is how it feels to everyone in the circle. It can be amazingly powerful and moving when enacted in this manner.

On the other hand, if you do not have three women in your group who feel comfortable doing this, it will still work reasonably well if most of the ritual is read by one High Priestess, as usual. If you do not have a High Priest, the High Priestess, another group member, or a visiting male participant can invoke the god.

supplies:

❑ Bonfire (if possible)

❑ Small candles to place around the outside of the circle (tea lights in white or orange work well.)

❑ Medium to large cauldron (the size depends on how many people you will have. Fill it with sand and stand white tapers in the sand.)

- ❑ One black taper candle
- ❑ Anointing oil
- ❑ Broom (also called a besom), if desired
- ❑ Optional: feather
- ❑ Optional: flaming torches to cast enough light for reading, if you are not holding the ritual in a well-lit area

· · ·

- Pre-ritual prep: Start the bonfire, light candles around the circle, and place the cauldron with candles in the center of the circle away from the bonfire (with the candles unlit). Set up the altar as usual, with both god and goddess candles (they can be black, if you want.)
- Participants should walk in a silent procession into the circle. As people enter, a group member should anoint them with oil, and another member can ring a bell or strike a chime as each person enters the circle. Otherwise, there should be silence.
- All enter the circle. The group members who are acting as Maiden, Mother, and Crone stand together by the altar.

Crone:

(walks around the outside of the circle with broom)

We sweep away all negativity from this circle and from ourselves. We release all negativity from our thoughts. Within this circle, only positive energy remains. We are safe and guarded within this sacred space.

Maiden:

(walks around the outside of the circle sprinkling a mixture of salt and water)

We purify the circle with salt and water.

Mother:

(walks around the outside of the circle with lit sage, wafting with a feather if you have one)

We purify the circle with fire and air.

Crone:

(walks around the outside of the circle with an athame or sword)

I cast the circle round and round, from Earth to sky, from sky to ground. I conjure now this sacred place, outside time and outside space. The circle is cast; we are between the worlds.

- Call the quarters.

High Priest:

Cernunnos, Lord of the Underworld, Keeper of the Darkness, come to us on this Samhain night. Walk with our ancestors from the lands where they now reside and join us in our celebration of life and death as we honor the great Wheel, ever turning. Cernunnos, we welcome you!

M/M/C:

(Maiden, Mother, and Crone speak together)

Hecate! Hear us! We invoke the triple goddess: Maiden, Mother, and Crone. Come to us on this Samhain Eve, as the veil between the world of the living and the world of the dead grows thin. Assist our loved ones who have gone before in returning to this earthly plane. Come be with your children this night. Hecate, we welcome you!

Crone:

We are at the crack of time. For this night belongs neither to the old year nor to the new. As there is no distinction between the years, there is no distinction between the world of the living and the world of the dead. Those we have loved and known in the past are free to return to us this night, here in this meeting place. We gather to honor them on this Samhain night.

Maiden:

As we begin our new year, know that with the turning of the wheel there is no end and no beginning. All is a continuous turning, a spiraling dance that moves ever on.

Mother:

As we are all part of the great Wheel, so we are all part of the goddess and god, who are with us always.

Maiden:

We are Maiden.

Mother:

We are Mother.

Crone:

We are Crone.

M/M/C:

We are many, but we are one.

Maiden:

It is Samhain, the Witches' New Year.

Mother:

It is Samhain, when the veil between the worlds is thin.

Crone:

Tonight we say goodbye to those we have lost. Tonight we start anew, and look to the future. Tonight, all things are possible.

M/M/C:

We are Maiden; we are Mother; we are Crone.

Maiden:

We are the hope for a new day.

Mother:

We are the comfort of hearth and home.

Crone:

We are wisdom in the twilight years.

M/M/C:

We are the beginning and the end. From us all things come, and to us all things must return.

Maiden:

Death is not an end, but a new beginning.

Mother:

And yet, it is only human to mourn what has been lost.

Crone:

Tonight, while the veil is thin, you may speak of loved ones past, and say goodbye.

- Crone lights black candle from goddess candle, passes it to the first participant; it is a good idea to tell this person what to do, so they can set an example. As the candle is passed around the circle, each person goes to the cauldron and lights a candle for one they lost—speaking the name of the person out loud if they choose, and then giving the main candle to the next person. Mother/Maiden/Crone go last.

M/M/C:

Now there is light where before there was darkness. We give freely of our love, that all may heal. So mote it be.

Maiden:

We are Maiden.

Mother:

We are Mother.

Crone:

We are Crone.

M/M/C:

We are many, and we are one.

[Pause]

Maiden:

We welcome in the New Year, and bid you rejoice.

Mother:

We give the gift of new beginnings, and grant you wishes three.

Crone:

So think upon what you desire, and come before us with your wishes for the year ahead. (Again, start with a member who has been prepared to demonstrate.)

Each person takes a turn kneeling before the three High Priestesses, and says:

Goddess, I ask that you grant me these boons three—_____. (Each person names three things—prosperity, peace, or the like.)

M/M/C:

(Hold hands out in blessing)

So you will it, and so mote it be.

(Repeat for all. When the others are done, the Maiden kneels before Mother, the Mother kneels before the Crone, and the Crone kneels before the Maiden.)

M/M/C:

As we will it, so mote it be

Start chanting:

We are the old people; We are the new people; We are the same people, stronger than before.

If you don't know the tune to this one, you can use another chant, or else chant this one without a tune. Chant, drum, and dance around the circle to raise the cone of power.

As the power peaks, the three HPS return to front and raise their arms.

M/M/C:

We have raised the cone of power. We take what we need and send the rest out into the Universe.

They can let out a big yell, or beat a drum hard to signal the letting go of the energy. Ground.

- Moment of Silence.

Crone (holding out cakes):

Bless these cakes, gift of the earth our Mother. May they nourish us as she does. (Crone passes cakes and says, "May the year to come be full of joy.")

Crone (holding out athame as the Maiden holds up a chalice and inserts athame into chalice while speaking): Let it be known that no man is greater than a woman, nor woman greater than a man. For what one lacks, the other can give. As the chalice is to the female, so the athame is to the male, and when they are joined it is magick in truth, for there is no greater magick in the world than love. (Crone passes chalice, saying, "May your life overflow with sweetness.")

Mother:

Speak now of what is in your heart, and know that we will always listen.

(Mother passes the speaking stick, starting with the first participant past HPS. The HPS can choose not to speak, if they feel it will disrupt their channeling of the goddess.)

- After all are done, have a moment of silence.

Maiden:

We are Maiden.

Mother:

We are Mother.

Crone:

We are Crone.

M/M/C:

And know this—if you find us not within you, you shall never find us without. For love is the law, and love is the bond. (pause) We give you bright blessings.

- Dismiss the quarters (reverse of start).

Crone:

Great Goddess Hecate! We give our thanks to you for being with us here in this sacred space. As the new year begins and the worlds of the living and dead once again separate, we ask that you guide our ancestors back to the Summerlands as you guide us in our everyday life. May you bring love and beauty to the world through us. In perfect love and perfect trust, so mote it be!

High Priest:

Great God Cernunnos! God of darkness and night—as the new year begins and as the cold of winter falls upon us, we ask that you guide us through the darkness and watch over us until the light returns again. In perfect love and perfect trust, so mote it be!

- All join hands, and recite the Wiccan Rede:

Bide the Wiccan law we must

In perfect love and perfect trust

Eight words the Wiccan Rede fulfill

An it harm none, do as ye will

Lest in thy self defense it be

Ever mind the law of three

Follow this with mind and heart
And merrie ye meet, and merrie ye part!
The circle is open, but never broken.

October New Moon

Gemstone Magick ritual

Gemstones are another important component of a Witch's tool kit. The stones are believed to be endowed with certain innate powers, which vary with the stone (and which Witch you ask, as usual). For instance, malachite is good for prosperity work (as are most green stones), and black onyx is very protective. Psychics often wear a black onyx ring on their left hand to ward off negativity and the sometimes intrusive energy of those around them.

Gemstones are considered to represent Earth because of their obvious connections with that element. You can put a stone on your altar in the northern quarter, if you like. Even certain "gemstones" that are not really stones at all—like amber (dried tree resin) and mother of pearl (shell)—are used in the same way as true gemstones.

Most pagan and New Age stores carry a large variety of tumbled stones for spiritual use, or you can find them easily in online shops. You can also wear your gemstones in the form of jewelry, and many Witches have special necklaces that pair their favorite stones with a silver pentacle. In years past, Witches often wore necklaces made out of amber and jet, which were said to be the Witches' stones. Sadly, it is next to impossible to find jet these days, but you can substitute black onyx for much the same effect.

For this New Moon ritual, you are going to want to have at least one tumbled stone per person, and more if possible. When Blue Moon Circle did this one, everyone researched one kind of gemstone, and brought enough pieces of that stone for everyone—very similar to the New Moon we did on herbs. Doing so gives all your group members a lot of information without the need for any one person to do too much work, and it also allows everyone the chance to share and contribute.

suppLies:

❏ Tumbled gemstones (enough for everyone to have at least one). Some of my favorites for magickal use include:

> › Crystal quartz (which boosts all magick, as well as being protective, healing, and aiding psychic work)

> › Amethyst (healing, dreams, psychic powers, peace, love, courage, happiness, and protection—one of the best good-for-everything stones)

> › Carnelian (protection, peace, energy, balance, healing, courage)

> › Tigerseye (money, protection, courage, luck, energy, power)

> › Black onyx (protection)

❏ But you can use whichever ones appeal to you!

❏ You can also bring with you to circle any jewelry that is customarily worn while doing magick.

❏ Be sure to bring your Book of Shadows.

You should also bring any research your group has done on stones, or a few books on magickal gemstone use. Every Witch should have at least one book on the use of stones, one on candles, one on herbs, and so forth, as well as a few books that contain information on a number of magickal tools and their uses. Information is power, and books are one of your most powerful tools. If you are just starting out, and don't have a lot of books, you can try checking one of the many Wiccan sites online; many of them have a wide range of information.

• • •

- Consecrate and cleanse the circle by passing sage or incense.
- Consecrate and cleanse the circle by passing salt and water.
- Cast the circle hand to hand or by having the HPS walk around the outside of the circle with her athame or sword.
- Call the quarters. You may want to say something like this when you call North: "I call the watchtower of the North, the power of Earth. Help us to find the strength in these stones that we have gathered for our magickal work, and enable us to use their energies wisely."
- HPS invokes the goddess.

- Sit in circle and share the information you have gathered about gemstones. If you did not do any research ahead of time, share the information in the books you have brought. Talk about your favorite stones, and which ones you are drawn to the most (not always the same thing). Write what you have learned in your Books of Shadows. Here are a couple to get you started:

Crystal quartz

This stone has a long history of shamanic and spiritual use, and is a favorite of Native Americans. It is often used in charm bags, and on top of staffs and wands. It symbolizes water, spirit, and the intellect. It also represents the goddess, and so is used at many New Moon and Full Moon rituals. Many Witches keep a large chunk of crystal on their altars. Crystal quartz is used in both defensive and protective magick. It has very strong healing properties, and has traditionally been carried to increase psychic abilities and for scrying (hence the Witch's "crystal ball"). Crystals can be cleared of negative energy by holding them in running water or by putting them out under a Full Moon.

Amethyst

Amethyst is one of the most all-around powerful stones used in magick. Found in various shades of purple, its history as a magickal and spiritual tool goes back thousands of years. Often used to symbolize love, amethyst has no negative qualities, and is often exchanged between lovers and used in spells to magnify beauty. It is associated with dreams, and is used to drive away both insomnia and nightmares, and to bring on prophetic dreaming. Amethyst calms and de-stresses, lends courage to those who wear it, protects travelers against sickness and danger, and aids meditation. It is used for divinatory magick (some Witches keep an amethyst with their tarot cards), and for all types of healing work.

- Once the group has finished its discussion, everyone should lay their stones (and jewelry, if they have brought any) on the altar. Focus on the stones and on your intention to bring out all their hidden potential. Think about using them in future magickal work; you might visualize yourself placing one on your altar, or in a charm bag. When you are all ready, say the following spell together:

gemstone magick speLL

Lapis blue and Turquoise healing

Amethyst and Quartz revealing

Onyx black will keep from harm

Hematite to ground our charm

Quartz of rose for friends and love

Moonstone's Lady's up above

Malachite will bring us wealth

Bloodstone, Agate, Jade for health

Jet and Amber, our delight

As we meet in darkest night

Stones of Earth, stones of power

Serve us in this magick hour

(Repeat three times for added power)

So mote it be

• • •

- Pick up the stones and feel the magick coursing through them. Ground and center.
- Pass cakes and ale (rock candy, anyone?)
- Pass the speaking stick.
- Dismiss the quarters.
- HPS thanks the goddess.
- Open the circle.

October Full Moon

Opening the inner eye

As we move indoors for the colder weather, we also turn our attentions inward. The October Full Moon, preceding Samhain, is ideal for working on prophecy and inner vision. As the veil between the worlds grows thinner, it becomes easier to see that which is normally unseen, and to hear the quiet inner voice that sometimes guides us.

Witches have historically used various forms of divination, including tarot cards, rune stones, scrying mirrors, and crystal balls. All of these tools help us to access our sixth sense, which moves in areas beyond the normal five. Not all Witches are psychic nor are all psychics Witches—but it is not uncommon for those who are drawn to Wicca to also have a gift for working with the tools of divination.

If those in your group do not have tarot cards or rune stones, now is the perfect time to get them, and to start to develop a feel for using them. Some Witches are more comfortable with one tool than another, and some use them all. There are even a few folks who are uneasy with the whole idea; such people can just observe and learn, if that is what they wish. Never force anyone in your group to do anything that makes them uncomfortable.

For this ritual, the members of Blue Moon Circle used tarot cards, since we all had them—even though some of us had been reading cards for years (one professionally), and two had just started. If the members of your group don't want to get tarot cards, they can easily buy or make their own rune stones, and use those instead.

The main focus of this Full Moon ritual is on opening the inner eye (or vision) so that we can see more clearly, but there is also a small blessing for use in consecrating your cards or stones. This blessing can also be used during other rituals to consecrate additional tools for magickal use.

SuppLies:

❏ Tarot cards or rune stones (preferably one set for each member in the group, although you can share if you need to do so.)

❏ Magickal oil (good ones to use for divination include lemongrass, sage, patchouli, and sandalwood, but you can use whatever makes you feel relaxed and centered.)

• • •

- Consecrate and cleanse the circle by passing sage or incense.
- Consecrate and cleanse the circle by passing salt and water.
- Cast the circle hand to hand.
- Call the quarters. (If you like, you can ask Air for help with psychic powers, Fire for help with courage in facing the unknown, Water for help with intuition, and Earth for help staying grounded and focused during the work.)
- HPS invokes the goddess (Full Moon invocation).
- If desired, this is a good time to read *The Charge of the Goddess*.
- Sit in the circle and get comfortable. Discuss past experiences with the cards—or whatever tools you are using for this ritual—and divination. If anyone has new tarot cards or rune stones, the HPS can use the following blessing (also found in the February chapter) to consecrate them:

tool consecration blessing

Great Goddess, bless these cards (or stones)

That they may be used for good and never harm

That they may help me in my Craft

And aid me in my magickal work

From this day forward

May they be blessed and consecrated

By the power of Earth (sprinkle tool with salt)

By the power of Air (waft with feather, incense or sage)

By the power of Fire (pass tool over candle)

And the power of Water (sprinkle tool with water)

And by the power of the spirit which lies within us all

So mote it be

• • •

- Take turns going around the circle and doing a reading for each other. It is fine for the more experienced readers to help out any members who are still unsure of what they are doing. You are tuning in to the cards (or stones) during this part of the ritual, but you can also be having fun!

- Once you have each had a turn, you can do the following spell to open your inner vision even more. In the future, you can do this spell any time you are in need of guidance—although you may find that it was so effective the first time that you never have to repeat it.

- Pass the magickal oil around the circle, and place a drop on your third eye (between the eyebrows, thought to be the center of psychic power) *or* take turns around the circle placing the oil on each other. When you are finished, focus and say this spell:

spell to open the inner eye

Moon, Moon, burning bright

Help me hone my inner sight

Make my vision clear and true

Show me what I need to do

Whether cards or stones of old

Show me what I need to know

Guide my heart and guide my hand

Help me see and understand

So mote it be

• • •

- Pass cakes and ale.
- Pass the speaking stick.
- Dismiss the quarters.
- HPS thanks the goddess.
- Open the circle.

❧ Notes

_____   _____
_____   _____
_____   _____
_____   _____
_____   _____
_____   _____
_____   _____
_____   _____
_____   _____
_____   _____
_____   _____
_____   _____
_____   _____
_____   _____
_____   _____
_____   _____

chapter 14

November

November can be a challenging month. Winter is setting in. The days are shorter, the nights are longer, and there is less light. It is natural for our bodies to start to slow down. We grow a bit sluggish, and it gets just a little harder to get out of bed in the morning.

As Wiccans, we try to go with the flow of the changing seasons. It is probably not a bad idea to get a little more sleep, and to slow down some if you can. Unfortunately, our modern existence doesn't often take the natural cycles of life into consideration. And other than eating a little extra chocolate, there doesn't always seem to be a healthy way to perk ourselves up so that we can keep up with the pace of our still-hectic lives.

Luckily, as Witches, we can always ask the gods for a little boost. The New Moon spell in this chapter is designed to "recharge our batteries" in as healthy a way as possible, while still respecting the quieter aspects of this segment of the Wheel of the Year.

November New Moon

Increasing energy spell

supplies:

❏ One red candle per person

❏ One tumbled stone per person (tigerseye is best, but carnelian or crystal quartz will do.)

❏ Small glass bottles or vials to put oil in

❏ A base oil—either olive oil from the kitchen, or an oil from the health or body-care section of a local health food store (sesame and grapeseed are nice, and fairly easy to find.)

❏ Essential oils: ginger, orange, and carnation (if you cannot find one of these, you may substitute sage or peppermint oils. Those that come with droppers are easiest to use.)

❏ Optional: red carnations for the altar

❏ Optional: a small funnel

Note: This spell combines candle magick, stone magick, and plant magick for extra power. If necessary, it can be done with only two of the three elements (if you can't find the stones, for instance).

• • •

• Consecrate and cleanse the circle with sage or incense (if using incense, carnation, ginger, or something else with a spicy smell would be best—no relaxing lavender here.)

• Consecrate and cleanse the circle with salt and water.

• Cast the circle hand to hand or by having the HPS walk around the outside with her athame or sword.

• Call the quarters.

HPS invokes the goddess:

Great Goddess, you who are warmth in the midst of the coldest days and a glowing light within the darkest hour, come to us in our circle. Help us to find the energy of the summer's sun despite the winter's chill and gloom. Welcome, and blessed be.

- Sit down around a table and make yourselves comfortable. You may want to talk a little about how having less energy affects your lives, and what you would accomplish if you had more energy.

- Take the small vials and pour some of the base oil into them (the small funnel is useful here), to about three quarters full.

- Pass the essential oils around the table and put a few drops of each into your individual vials or bottles. While you are dropping in the oils, visualize the energy of the sun going into the plants and the energy of the plants going into the oils. Feel the summer sun on your face and the roots of the plant digging into the soil. Concentrate as hard as you can on the powers that are locked up inside every drop of essential oil.

- When you have combined the essential oils and the base oil, put the cap on your bottle, close your eyes and shake gently to mix. Hold the bottle tightly in your hands. Visualize the oils coming together and becoming even more powerful together than they were individually. See your bottle beginning to glow with light and power, with red or golden light streaming from between your fingers.

- Open your eyes and take a stone and a candle from the altar. Anoint each with a few drops of the energy oil you have just made. You can anoint yourself too—between the eyes and over the heart and the belly—if you wish.

- Visualize the candle and the stone glowing with energy as you did with the oil.

- Now, visualize yourself glowing with energy too, and recite the spell together:

spell for energy

I call upon the Power of Air, with energy creative

I call upon the Power of Fire, with energy passionate

I call upon the Power of Water, with energy healing

I call upon the Power of Earth, with energy strong and unending

I call upon my inner wisdom

That I may tap into this energy only when it is needed

And rest when rest is called for

Let the energy be there for me when I need it

Let the energy be there for me when I call it

Let the energy be there for me when I will it

So mote it be

• • •

- Sit for a moment and absorb the energy. Then ground and let any excess go into the floor.
- You can light your candle now, or save it for later. The stone can be carried with you or placed on your altar. Whenever you need extra energy, say the spell again or just anoint yourself with a drop or two of the oil.
- Pass cakes and ale.
- Pass the speaking stick.

- Dismiss the quarters.
- HPS thanks the goddess.
- Open the circle.

November Full Moon

Faith and gratitude spell

We often ask the gods for help. This is not a bad thing. It is, in fact, a great part of being a Witch—knowing that we can ask and that frequently we are granted the thing we have asked for (even if not always in the ways we expected). But we should be careful of falling into the habit of only talking to the ancient gods when we want something from them.

Sometimes it is good to just say "thank you." I try to remember, whenever I stand before my altar, to start out by thanking the goddess and god for the blessings of that day, or week, or my life in general. Only after I have done so do I proceed with any spells or requests that I might have.

November is a good time to give this issue some thought. Most of us celebrate Thanksgiving in one form or another, and therefore we may already be more conscious than usual of the importance of giving thanks for the good things in our lives. So it seems appropriate to set aside the Full Moon ritual in this month for a focus on gratitude and appreciation.

Wiccans tend to look at the "gifts" in our lives a little differently from most people. For the most part, we believe in reincarnation. We believe that the lives that we lead are filled with experiences from which we will learn and grow so that in the next life we can move on to the next lesson. These experiences are often unpleasant and challenging. Many are painful. And yet, because we know they serve a purpose, we know that these difficult experiences can be as much a gift as prosperity and good health.

This can be a difficult point to remember while you are in the midst of crisis and struggling with day-to-day problems. It is usually only in hindsight that we can clearly see the benefits we derived from the hard lessons with which we were "gifted."

So, at November's Full Moon, we pause to look back at the gifts we have been given—the obvious and the not-so-obvious—to give thanks to the gods, and to remind ourselves that sometimes life just has to be taken on faith. For that, too, is a part of being a Witch.

supplies:

- ❏ Large white or gold candle
- ❏ Anointing oil (you can use the peace and happiness oil from February if you have it, or any other magickal oil you think is suitable—plain sage or lavender is fine, too.)
- ❏ Slips of paper and pencils

• • •

- Consecrate and cleanse the circle with sage or incense.
- Consecrate and cleanse the circle with salt and water.
- Cast the circle hand to hand.
- Call the quarters.
- HPS invokes the goddess (Full Moon invocation—see chapter 17.)
- HPS or other female group member reads *The Charge of the Goddess*.
- Sit comfortably and talk a little bit about the things in your lives that you are grateful for. Remember to include the challenges as well as the obvious pleasures. Then, each person should sit quietly and write up a list of everything for which they are thankful. The list may include some or all of the following: friends, family, a significant other, pets, home, food, job, health, money, intelligence, courage, good weather, your Wiccan practice, happiness, an hour of quiet away from your children. Include anything you can think of that you are thankful for. Take as long for this as everyone needs, as this part of the ritual is just as important as saying the actual spell.
- When your lists are complete, light the gratitude candle and recite the spell (you can put a copy of the spell down in front of you and hold hands if you want.)

faith and gratitude spell

We come in thanks and gratitude

In humbleness and awe

With grateful heart and somber mood

And mindful of the Law

The little gifts we've given out

Returned to us by three

Remind us to let go of doubt

And say, "So mote it be"

In faith we've come before the gods

In love they've sent us back

With answered prayers against all odds

And gifts of what we lack

Help our faith be true and strong

To remember gratitude as well

And send our love and thanks along

With each and every spell

So mote it be

- Take a deep breath and send your thanks out to the gods. Focus on your intent to remember to say "thank you."
- Pass cakes and ale.
- Pass the speaking stick.
- Dismiss the quarters.
- HPS thanks the goddess.
- Open the circle by reciting the Wiccan Rede:

Bide the Wiccan Law ye must

In perfect love and perfect trust

Eight words the Wiccan Rede fulfill

An it harm none, do as ye will

Lest in thy self defense it be

Ever mind the law of three

Follow this with mind and heart

And merrie ye meet and merrie ye part

✺ Notes

_____   _____
_____   _____
_____   _____
_____   _____
_____   _____
_____   _____
_____   _____
_____   _____
_____   _____
_____   _____
_____   _____
_____   _____
_____   _____
_____   _____
_____   _____
_____   _____
_____   _____
_____   _____

CHAPTER 15

December

December is a month for holiday celebrations, no matter which religion you follow. For Pagans, that holiday is Yule, which falls on or around December twenty-first. Yule is a celebration of the Winter Solstice, the longest night of the year.

In the Wiccan symbolism of the turning Wheel of the Year, this is the time when the Holly King (who represents the dark half of the year) is overthrown by the Oak King (who represents the light half of the year), thus ensuring the slow return of light and warmth. The goddess, as Mother, gives birth to the infant god, completing the cycle of birth, growth, death, and rebirth. Hope is born again.

Wiccans celebrate Yule by making wreaths of pine boughs or holly, or by bringing a small living tree indoors and decorating it with apples, cinnamon sticks, or popcorn to feed the wood sprites that might come in with it. Fir trees are traditional because they are symbolic of the "life in the midst of death" aspect of the season, since they remain green when most other trees are bare.

We kindle bonfires and light lots of candles to represent the return of the light, and burn a Yule log for good fortune in the coming year.

Clearly, many of the traditions most people associate with Christmas are rooted in the pagan festivities of Yule. The tree, wreaths, holly, and mistletoe are familiar pagan symbols, and the Christmas colors of green and red come from these as well. The five-pointed star on top of the tree is derived from the pentacle that symbolizes the five elements of Earth, Air, Fire, Water, and Spirit. Even Santa Claus—the Oak King in another guise—brings gifts to represent the prosperity of the coming year.

Because of the many similarities between the two holidays, many Wiccans choose this time of year to share their pagan celebrations with their non-pagan friends. People who might be uncomfortable coming to a ritual may be quite happy to be invited to a Winter Solstice party.

Blue Moon Circle uses this time to include the significant others of our group members. Often, family and friends attend as well. Rather than have a Full Moon ritual, we often have a Solstice feast instead, and simply enjoy the holiday and the pleasure of being able to share it with the ones we love.

Yule ritual

suppLies:

❏ Bag or basket with small gifts, enough for everyone (these can be packets of incense, candles, small statues—anything that would appeal to most people and cost very little. A local dollar store is a great place to find such things.)

❏ A Yule tree, if you want to use one

❏ Drums

Of all the holidays of the year, Yule seems to be the easiest to share with non-pagan friends and family—maybe because so much of it is so familiar to them. This ritual is written with that in mind, and takes into consideration the possibility of guests who might be less familiar with ritual in general. Therefore, there is more explanation than usual. Feel free to leave some of the explanatory passages out if they aren't necessary for your group's ritual.

• • •

HPS/HP:

Welcome to our celebration of the Winter Solstice, also known as Yule. Today is the shortest day of the year and the longest night. Tonight the darkness rules. Yet we rejoice in the light to come as each day moves us toward the spring and new growth. We come together to celebrate the turning of the cosmic Wheel, a constant cycle of dark and light, death and rebirth, where nothing is ever lost, and all things have their proper time and place. Tonight we rejoice together. (Group members beat drums for a minute.)

HPS/HP:

We will now cast our circle and create a sacred space. We purify the circle with sage, representing the elements of Fire and Air.

• Group member walks around the circle with sage.

HPS/HP:

We purify the circle with salt and with water, representing the elements of Earth and Water.

• Circle member walks around the circle with salt and water.

HPS/HP:

Next, we summon the spirits of the four quarters to guard us.

Group member calls East:

Watchtower of the East, element of Air, join us in our circle, and watch over us as we celebrate. Blow away all negativity, and leave us feeling clear and centered. Welcome, and blessed be. (Light yellow candle.)

Group member calls South:

Watchtower of the South, element of Fire, join us in our circle and watch over us as we celebrate. Burn away stress and turmoil, leaving us filled with the joy of the season. Welcome, and blessed be. (Light red candle.)

Group member calls West:

Watchtower of the West, element of Water, join us in our circle and watch over us as we celebrate. Wash away our doubts and fears, and leave us open to new possibilities. Welcome, and blessed be. (Light blue candle.)

Group member calls North:

Watchtower of the North, element of Earth, join us in our circle and watch over us as we celebrate. Help us to be grounded and firm in our intentions. Welcome, and blessed be. (Light green candle.)

HPS invokes the goddess:

I invoke the goddess, gracious lady of the moon, from whom all blessings flow. At Yule, we celebrate you in your guise as Mother, bringing us your gift of a new son and hope for the future. Surround us with your love as we celebrate this rite in your honor. Welcome, and blessed be.

HP invokes the god:

I invoke the god, King of Oak and of Holly. You grew old in the service of your people, and now you are reborn again. Share with us the wisdom of the old king, and the youthful energy of the new as we celebrate this rite in your honor. Welcome, and blessed be.

HPS/HP:

Hand to hand I cast the circle. (Hands are joined around circle.) The circle is cast; we are between the worlds. This is a sacred space, outside of time, where we are joined in perfect love, and perfect trust. Let all we do within this space be for good. So mote it be.

HPS/HP:

Winter Solstice is a day celebrated by many different cultures throughout history. Even Christianity adopted many of the pagan elements of Yule, such as the Yule tree or Yule log, and the symbolic kindling of lights that has evolved into the lights hung upon the Christmas tree. All through the world people have historically observed this important day in the cycle of the yearly Wheel.

HPS/HP:

One thing that almost all cultures have in common is the giving of gifts! (Enthusiastic drumming. Yells of joy). We will now pass out these small gifts to you, as a memento of our time here together. (Group member walks around the circle handing out gifts.)

HPS/HP:

Of course, there are many important gifts that are less tangible than these.

Group member:

There is the gift of family and friends.

Group member:

There is the gift of a day to spend together with those we love and cherish.

Group member:

There are the gifts of health, of prosperity, of knowledge, and of joy. (If you have more members, this can be split up further.)

Group member:

There is the gift of love.

HPS/HP:

And there is a gift that we traditionally ask for at this time of year—peace on Earth, and goodwill toward all. In these troubled days, we need this gift more than ever. So, tonight we will join together and cast a spell for peace. A spell is much like a wish or a prayer—it is intent made manifest. We focus our will, and send that power out into the universe to create positive change. And in doing so, we pledge our commitment to work toward that change. Any spell is powerful. Working together in this sacred space, with all our energies focused on the same goal, who knows what we can achieve?

Now we raise energy by drumming, by clapping, by dancing. As we do these things, let us focus our thoughts on our goal tonight, the goal of peace. When the time is right, and the power is at its peak, we will stop drumming and recite the spell together. After the spell, we will ground ourselves, releasing the energy we have built up into the earth below.

- Circle members drum, clap, and stomp their feet. When the energy reaches its peak, HPS beats drum hard to signal everyone to stop. Then she leads the group in reciting the spell:

Great Goddess, Great God, please grant this boon

Bring us peace, and bring it soon

With winter's quiet and snow's pure fall

Bring peace to the world and joy to all

With each white flake let love give birth

Bringing calm, serenity, and peace on Earth

So mote it be

• • •

- Ground by touching hands to the floor to discharge any excess energy. Hug and kiss, if everyone is comfortable with that.
- Pass cakes and ale. Cider or mulled wine are perfect for this holiday, as are decorated cookies.
- Pass the speaking stick.

HPS/HP:

This is the time that we pass the speaking stick. Each person will have a chance to talk about gifts they would like to receive, and those they would like to give in the coming year. If you don't wish to speak, that's fine. (HPS starts. Examples: "I'd like to receive the gifts of health, prosperity, and love. I'd like to give the gifts of compassion and patience.")

- Dismiss the quarters. ("I thank the Guardian of the East for watching over our circle. Farewell, and blessed be," and so forth.)

HP thanks the god:

Great Oak King, we thank you for joining us in our celebration tonight. May your reign be easy—and brief! Farewell, and blessed be.

HPS thanks the goddess:

Great Goddess, you who are Mother of us all, we thank you for your presence here, tonight and always. Farewell and blessed be.

- All join hands.

HPS/HP says:

The circle is open but never broken. Merrie meet, merrie part, and merrie meet again! (Raise hands into the air, and then let go of each other. The circle is opened.)

December New Moon

Crafting a Yule wreath

The Yule wreath is a perfect symbol for the season. Its circular form represents the never-ending cycle of life and death, and the evergreens, holly and other plants remind us that life continues in the midst of the winter cold and dark. You can even tuck in a piece of mistletoe, if you want to add a bit of romance!

Although practicing magick is often a serious business, sometimes it is nice just to relax and have a little fun. Reverence and mirth, after all—they both have their place. So, for the December New Moon, Blue Moon Circle takes a break from the serious work of crafting magick and crafts a wreath together instead.

Not only is this an enjoyable and entertaining way to pass the time, but it also gives us a chance to chat, play, and to get to know each other better—something that is often difficult to do in the midst of the more intense practice of our Craft.

supplies:

❏ One wreath base (this base can be made from willow, or any other twisted wood or vine; it should be easy to find at your local craft store, or any large "supercenter"-type store)

❏ Freshly cut evergreen boughs (you can always cut these off of a small Christmas tree if you don't have any evergreens growing near you and can't find pre-cut evergreens at your local florist.)

❏ Holly, mistletoe, herbs (rosemary is especially nice—any living plant that lasts for a while when cut will do, even flowers like roses or carnations in seasonal colors.)

❏ Pinecones

❏ Cinnamon sticks

❏ Lightweight wire (like florist's wire)

❏ Flat ribbons in red, green, and gold

❏ Permanent ink fine/medium point marker

❏ A glue gun might be helpful, but you can do without one.

Note: If you really want to be relaxed about this, you can skip casting the circle on this occasion. If you like, enjoy some mulled cider or wine and a cookie or two while you're working (to keep your strength up . . .)

. . .

- Consecrate and cleanse the circle with sage or incense.

- Consecrate and cleanse the circle with salt and water.

- Cast the circle hand to hand.

- Call the quarters.

- HPS invokes the goddess.

- Gather together all your supplies in the middle of your circle (this may be easiest to do around a small table.)

- Take turns passing the wreath form around the circle, and tucking in pieces of pine bough.

- When the wreath is mostly filled in, take your marker and write your wishes for the coming year on some of the ribbons. Take turns winding your ribbons in and out of the wreath. (If you want them to be more hidden, you can start with this step.)

- Once the evergreens and ribbons are complete, pass the wreath around the circle and let everyone take turns placing the other items wherever they like on the front of the wreath. You can use the wire or glue to help them stay on, which is especially helpful with the pinecones and pieces of cinnamon. Don't forget to think about what your symbols mean and why you are making the wreath, but do remember to have fun and don't worry too much about making it look perfect.

- When it is done, you can hang some more ribbons around the bottom part of the wreath. (You can write the name of your group on these if you want, or more wishes, or leave them blank.)

- If desired, you can bless and consecrate the wreath when it is done. This step is nice, but not really necessary—it is already filled with positive energy by the act of working together and the love and friendship you shared while making it.

- Pass cakes and ale. Hot cider or mulled wine are perfect.

- Pass the speaking stick.

- Dismiss the quarters.

- Thank the goddess.

- Open the circle.

Note: You can hang the wreath wherever you meet the most often, or you can share it. Be sure to display it at your Winter Solstice feast, if you have one.

December Full Moon

Winter Solstice feast

December is a hectic month for most of us. Even the most dedicated Pagan is often pulled into the traditional holiday celebrations of Thanksgiving (in North America) and Christmas or Hanukkah, due to connections to non-Pagan family and friends. And work can be crazy too—especially if you're in retail! Many of us end up juggling family, travel, and business obligations, any of which can be overwhelming.

As you could tell from the introduction to this chapter, Blue Moon Circle deals with all this in a very Wiccan way—we have a party.

Winter Solstice, even more than most pagan holidays, is a traditional time for feasting. We come together in warmth during a time of cold and create a light in the darkness with revelry and fun. It is the perfect time to include your family and friends in a non-threatening pagan celebration, especially if your significant others are generally not comfortable attending rituals.

There is no right or wrong way of doing this. You can invite a few people or many, include kids or not as you choose, keep it casual, or get all dressed up in your holiday best. Blue Moon Circle celebrates with an adults-only, semi-formal dinner party, complete with a gift-giving game, but you and your group will probably come up with Solstice traditions of your own.

Meanwhile, the following is a description of the Blue Moon Circle Winter Solstice feast to use as a guide for your own festivities. If you started this book in January, you have now completed a full year of Wiccan group practice—and that in itself is cause for celebration! If not, then you still have much to look forward to. The members of Blue Moon Circle join me in wishing you and yours a very magickal year to come!

- Send out fancy invitations at least three weeks in advance—even to the members of your own group. (It's fun to get an invitation to a party in the mail.) Be sure to specify who is invited, and whether or not children are welcome. If the feast is going to be potluck (and it is far easier on whoever is hosting it to have everyone bring something), discuss ahead of time who is bringing what, who will be responsible for sending out invitations, making decorations, and so on.

- If you are playing the gift-giving game, be sure and tell people to bring one gift per person attending (if two people are coming, they need to bring two gifts.) Gifts should be wrapped. It is a good idea to have a few extra gifts on hand in case someone forgets to bring one.

- The night of the feast, decorate the house in which the party is being held with plenty of candles, your group wreath from New Moon, and other festive seasonal touches. Greenery swags, Yule trees, and pinecones are all nice ways to bring nature inside during a time when it is too cold to celebrate outside. You can make the house smell festive too, by using scented candles, stovetop potpourri, or by hanging up oranges with cloves stuck into them.

- Participants should gather in a room where everyone can sit comfortably, more or less in a circle. At my house, this room is the living room, with some people sitting on the couches or on chairs dragged in from the dining room, and some sitting on pillows on the floor. If there are people who don't know each other, it is a good idea for all circle members and their guests to introduce themselves.

- Now is a perfect time to play the gift-giving game. It is a good ice breaker, and gets the party going without the usual awkward silences. The game is played as follows:

- Put out all the gifts within the circle at the feet of the giver. Gifts should be wrapped and should have cost no more than about ten U.S. dollars or any other pre-set amount. Gifts should be good for a man or a woman. Examples include small books such as *Llewellyn's Herbal Almanacs*, decorative boxes, crystals, seasonal ornaments, candles, chocolate, and other treats. Some of them should have a pagan theme, but probably not all.

- Ask everyone to write his or her name on a slip of paper, and put all the slips in a hat or bowl or a whimsical container of your choice.

- The person whose name is pulled out of the hat first picks one gift from all those in the circle. The gift is opened immediately, and shown to everyone.

- That person picks the next name out of the hat. The second person has the choice of picking any unopened gift from around the circle, or "stealing" the gift that the first person chosen. (I think you can see where this is going . . .)

- The second person picks out the name of the third person, and so on. Each one gets the option of choosing a new gift or "stealing" one that has already been opened. There is no limit to how many times a gift can be "stolen." Each person goes once. In the end, everyone ends up with one gift to take home, the floor is covered with scraps of wrapping paper, and the room is filled with laughter.

- Now it's time to feast! Be sure to serve seasonal foods like squash or pumpkin, root vegetables, and apples. Books with recipes for Wiccan holiday foods are available, too. (*Witch in the Kitchen* by Cait Johnson and *The Wicca Cookbook* by Jamie Wood and Tara Seefeldt are two great examples. See the Appendix C for details.) Corn bread, some form of roasted bird, and stuffed acorn squash are among the Blue Moon favorites. If vegetarians are coming, be sure to have plenty of options for them. Hot mulled cider and hot mulled wine are perfect for the occasion, or you can serve the traditional wassail.

- Wassail comes from the Anglo-Saxon toast "Wes hal!" ("Be in good health!"). Yule, traditionally a time for revelry and drinking, was outlawed by the Puritans for obvious reasons. Neighbors would go from house to house and be treated to wassail at every door. You can imagine what the group was like by the time they reached the last home in the village!

- Needless to say, wassail is traditionally made with alcohol (anything from bourbon to burgundy, depending on the recipe you follow), but you can always make a non-alcoholic wassail for the children's table, if there is one, or for those who would prefer not to imbibe.

- There are probably as many variations on the recipe for wassail as there are Pagans, but most of the recipes contain the following ingredients in one form or another:
    - Apple cider (approximately one gallon, or about four liters)
    - Wine, whiskey, or brandy (as much or as little as you like)
    - Various spices, often including allspice, cloves, cinnamon, and ginger. If you use whole pieces of the spices, they look pretty and are easier to fish out, so start with fewer and add more if needed.
    - Some form of sweetener, such as maple syrup or brown sugar (to taste)

- Mix them all together in a pot on the stove and heat until warm but not boiling. (Or use a slow cooker, if you have one.) If you want, slice an apple crosswise to reveal the pentacle shape on the inside, and float a few slices on top. Orange slices are pretty too.

- Don't forget to toast each other!

- And that's about it. Eat, drink, and be merry (but don't forget the designated drivers), and enjoy each other's company. Happy Solstice!

✐ Notes

_____   _____
_____   _____
_____   _____
_____   _____
_____   _____
_____   _____
_____   _____
_____   _____
_____   _____
_____   _____
_____   _____
_____   _____
_____   _____
_____   _____
_____   _____
_____   _____
_____   _____
_____   _____

part 3

more useful information

There are many great books available on just about any aspect of Wicca imaginable—and I suspect that, sooner or later, you will have as many as you can afford in your personal or group library. There is no way you can learn everything you need to know about herbal magick, stones, oils, holidays, history, or any other magick-related subject just by reading one book.

On the other hand, there is nothing more frustrating and annoying than having to search through eight or ten books just to find the one piece of information that you need to complete a ritual or project, especially when you are just getting started. So, it is nice to have some basic facts in one easy-to-find place.

Eventually, your Book of Shadows will probably be that place. Until then, I have compiled the essentials of magickal practice in this section. Here you will find the fundamentals of ritual etiquette, samples of quarter calls and god and goddess invocations, and some simple correspondences for use in spell crafting, along with other useful stuff.

Some of the rituals in this book already have quarter calls, invocations, and cakes-and-ale blessings written out within the ritual. In many of the New Moon and Full Moon rituals, these are left for you to fill in with the words of your choice. You can either make up your own (a good practice once you have more experience) or choose from among the options given in this section. Either way, unless everyone in the group has a copy of this book to read from, it is helpful to write quarter calls and other ritual words out ahead of time until you become more comfortable with them.

Remember that everything in this book, including the contents of this section, are only suggestions—words of advice from your friendly neighborhood High Priestess. Wicca is all about following your heart and listening to your own inner voice. If you are doing a spell that calls for a green candle, and your instinct tells you to use red, by all means do so.

This book and the information in this section are meant to be used only as a guide, and as a way to make your group practice easier and more fun. *So mote it be.*

CHAPTER 16

CIRCLE etiquette

This may well be the most important chapter in this book.

No, really. Although there is very little that all Wiccans agree upon, the truth is that the basics of circle etiquette found on these pages are an exception to that rule. Any circle you take part in will almost certainly follow these few rules:

- **Whenever you move around the circle, go in a clockwise direction (deosil).** The only exception is when you are doing banishing work, in which case you walk counterclockwise (widdershins).

- **Once the circle is cast, it should not be broken.** Once cast, the circle exists outside of time and space, and is a safe and sacred place. If you need to leave the circle space for any reason, you need to have someone "cut you out" of circle. (This is done by drawing a doorway with an athame or your finger, starting at the ground, going up and over, then down again. To cut someone back into the circle, draw the doorway in reverse.)

- **Never touch another Witch's tools without permission**. (Your circle may decide that this is fine, but always ask the first time.)

- **It is important to keep focus and concentration; there should be no "chit chat" during the main part of the ritual**. (Informal talking is okay during certain situations that require less intense focus, such as some of the craft project sections.)

- **Everything that is said in circle stays in circle**. It is crucial that the circle remain a safe place, in which all those in attendance feel free to speak what is in their hearts. This means that nothing said in confidence may ever be repeated. This also means that you should never tell anyone outside of circle any specifics of what occurred within, including the names of those who have attended a ritual. Not everyone is "out of the broom closet" and some people would rather not have others know they practice Witchcraft. This is one of the reasons that some Witches use "craft names" instead of real ones.

- **When the speaking stick is passed, only the person holding the stick may speak**. You will get your turn to talk when the stick comes around the circle. Be respectful of others and give your entire attention to whoever has the stick.

- **Show respect for the gods and the elements by standing during quarter calls and invocations, and turning with the rest of the circle to face the appropriate directions.** If you do not know what to do, you should just copy everyone else.

- **Show respect for the others in the circle.** Do not say negative things to others about those with whom you practice. Try not to judge or criticize.

- **Come to circle cleansed and prepared to do magickal work.** It is proper to bathe before rituals if at all possible. Never wear perfumes or colognes; many people are allergic or find the strong scents distracting. If possible, wear appropriate garb. Garb is any clothing you keep for magickal work—usually robes, fancy dresses, or cloaks. If you do not have garb, at least dress nicely. You wouldn't go to church in a torn t-shirt and muddy jeans. Don't show up for circle that way either.

- **Never come to circle under the influence of drugs or alcohol.** This is disrespectful to both the gods and your fellow circle members, and makes it next to impossible to build up energy in any productive way.

- **Do not ask personal questions of those participants whom you do not know well.** This is the privacy issue again. People will volunteer information (such as where they work) when they are ready.

These are the basics. Your circle may decide to establish rules of its own in addition to these. It is a good idea to make up a basic "ritual etiquette sheet" to give to any guests who have not previously attended rituals. At the very least, it may save someone from making an embarrassing blunder, and it might end up preventing a disaster—like the time that an inexperienced guest just got up and walked out of circle to go to the bathroom, and completely destroyed the energy we were trying to build up. (Poof! All gone.) An etiquette sheet will also make your guests more comfortable, since they will feel that they know what is expected of them.

As it says in the Wiccan Rede: follow this with mind and heart, and merrie ye meet and merrie ye part.

@ Notes

_____   _____
_____   _____
_____   _____
_____   _____
_____   _____
_____   _____
_____   _____
_____   _____
_____   _____
_____   _____
_____   _____
_____   _____
_____   _____
_____   _____
_____   _____
_____   _____

CHAPTER 17

RituaL eLements

At the beginning of Part 2, I talked about the basic components that make up a ritual: the welcoming speech (for larger rituals), cleansing and consecrating the space, casting the circle, calling the quarters, invoking the goddess and god, the main body of the ritual, cakes and ale, passing the speaking stick, dismissing the quarters, thanking the goddess and the god, and opening the circle.

Some of these components, like the welcoming speech, change with every ritual. These are all written out in each holiday ritual in this book and can be used as is or rewritten to suit your needs. Some, like the passing of the speaking stick, require no special words (other than the basic "Now we will pass the speaking stick").

All the rest, however, can be done in various ways. Some Witches always speak spontaneously, and never prepare anything ahead of time. Some Witches—like those of us in Blue Moon Circle—tend to speak from the heart and laugh at ourselves when we mess it up in our own private New Moon and Full

Moon gatherings, but write things out ahead of time for rituals to which we invite guests—especially those during which the guests may be inexperienced or unaccustomed to Wicca.

There is no right or wrong way. As I may have mentioned once or twice before, the gods are pretty flexible. But if you feel more comfortable in your early days of practicing as a group when you have the quarter calls written out on slips of paper so you can read them, by all means go ahead and write them. You can use the same calls every time, or you can use different ones for different occasions.

It is always helpful to have a copy of the spell you are doing written out for everyone—unless you are all reading it from this book, or it has already been written into everyone's Book of Shadows. As with everything else, the amount of preparation you do is up to you.

In this chapter, I will lay out a variety of options for quarter calls, invocations, and the rest. Some of these are already contained in a certain ritual. The holiday rituals included in the book usually have invocations to suit the occasion, but most New Moon and Full Moon descriptions just say—for example—"Call the quarters" and leave it up to you whether or not you want to do something spontaneous and unique to your group or use one of the options that I provide.

As you gain more and more experience with ritual practice, you will probably want your words to reflect the personality of your own group. But for now, here are some variations on the basics to give you a head start and to help you to become more comfortable with the words of ritual.

Casting the circle

- If you are casting the circle hand to hand, all you have to say is "I cast the circle hand to hand" one at a time as you go around the circle and take the hand of the person next to you. (HPS starts.)

- You can also cast the circle "heart to heart" by taking the next person's hand and holding it up to your heart.

- If the HPS or HP will be walking around the outside of the circle, and casting it with an athame or sword, I like to say the following: "I cast the circle round and round, from earth to sky, from sky to ground. I conjure now this sacred place, outside time and outside space. The circle is cast; we are between the worlds."

- It is always appropriate to say something like the following, no matter which way you cast the circle: "We are in a sacred space, between the worlds."

Calling the quarters

There are four quarters: North, East, South, and West. They have some basic correspondences and how we call them usually relates to these essentials. The quarters are also referred to as the elements (Earth, Air, Fire, and Water) or the watchtowers (because we call them to watch over the circle). Always make certain that you are facing in the correct direction when you call that quarter. A compass is a useful Witch tool, too.

Always call the quarters starting with East and proceeding clockwise. Dismiss the quarters starting with North and proceeding counterclockwise.

- *East*—the element of Air. Candle color is yellow. Tool is athame. Properties are intellect, knowledge, and psychic powers. It is often represented on the altar by incense or a feather.
- *South*—the element of Fire. Candle color is red. Tool is the wand. Properties are passion, courage, and energy. It is often represented on the altar by a candle.
- *West*—the element of Water. Candle color is blue. Tool is the chalice. Properties are emotions, intuition, and rebirth. It is often represented on the altar by a bowl of water, but some Witches use a seashell.
- *North*—the element of Earth. Candle color is green. Tool is the pentacle. Properties are grounding, focus, and the material world. It is often represented on the altar by salt or by a gemstone or everyday rock.

Quarter calls can be as simple or as complicated as you want them to be. The most basic call is as simple as "We call the power of East to come and guard our circle." The dismissal for this would then be "We thank the power of East for watching over our circle, and give it leave to go."

Most people use something a little bit more involved than this, although the dismissals tend to be somewhat simpler (if for no other reason than that people are often tired by the end of the ritual, or eager to get to the feasting). Here are some examples—for ease of use I have included a matching dismissal with each call:

Quarter call and dismissal #1

East

Optional: Light incense and say, "We summon the spirit of Air."

I call the watchtower of the East, the spirit of Air.

Help us to keep our minds clear and open, and aid us in seeking positive change.

Come now and guard our circle.

Spirit of Air, we thank you for your presence here in our circle.

You are free to go, although your essence is always with us.

Farewell and blessed be.

South

Optional: Throw sage on the bonfire and say, "We summon the spirit of Fire."

I call the watchtower of the South, the spirit of Fire.

Element of passion and transformation, help us to make the choices

That will lead to greater success in the months ahead.

Come now and guard our circle.

Spirit of Fire, we thank you for your presence here in our circle.

You are free to go, although your essence is always with us.

Farewell and blessed be.

West

Optional: Pour water on the ground and say, "We summon the spirit of Water."

I call the watchtower of the West, the spirit of Water.

Open our hearts to love, our bodies to healing and our minds to wisdom from within and without.

Come now and guard our circle.

Spirit of Water, we thank you for your presence here in our circle.

You are free to go, although your essence is always with us.

Farewell and blessed be.

North

Optional: Scatter salt on the ground and say, "We summon the spirit of Earth."

I call the watchtower of the North, the spirit of Earth.

Nourish and ground us; help us connect to all the hidden strengths within ourselves.

Come now and guard our circle.

Spirit of Earth, we thank you for your presence here in our circle.

You are free to go, although your essence is always with us.

Farewell, and blessed be.

Quarter call and dismissal #2

East

I summon the spirit of East, the element of Air, and bid you guard us with the power of the sudden storm and hold us safe with the gentleness of the evening breeze.

Air, element of the East, we thank you for your protection and grant you leave to go.

South

I summon the spirit of the South, the element of Fire, and bid you guard us with the power of the roaring flame and with the softly fading ember.

Fire, element of the South, we thank you for your protection and grant you leave to go.

West

I summon the spirit of the West, the element of Water, and bid you guard us with the power of the ocean waves and hold us safe like the waters of the Mother we all come from.

Water, element of the West, we thank you for your protection and grant you leave to go.

North

I summon the spirit of the North, the element of Earth, and bid you guard us with the strength of the land beneath our feet, and hold us like soil that nurtures the smallest seed.

Earth, element of the North, we thank you for your protection and grant you leave to go.

Invoking the god and goddess / Thanking the god and goddess

Like the quarter calls and dismissals, the god/goddess invocations are usually paired with a matching thanks. Also like the quarter calls, this farewell is often briefer and simpler than the invocation. Remember that although you summon the quarters to do your bidding, you always ask respectfully for the gods to attend you in your circle. After all, who are we to command the gods?

I have included the god and goddess invocations suitable to each holiday ritual in Part 2 in order to show you how they work. Sometimes a holiday has a specific deity (or deities) associated with it, in which case they are usually mentioned by name. Most Wiccans invoke both the god and goddess during holiday rituals.

In contrast, at the New Moon and Full Moon rituals, usually only the goddess is invoked. This is because the lunar celebrations are primarily her domain. You can also call the god if you want—there is no rule against it—but most Wiccans don't.

When you invoke the god and goddess, light a candle for each. Use white or silver for the goddess and yellow or gold for the god—or you can use white for both.

Some of the New Moons and Full Moons already have specific invocations included that mention the issues you will be working on during that ritual. For the rest, here are two examples:

New Moon goddess invocation #1

- Great Goddess, Lady of the Dark Moon, hear us! We your children gather here in sacred space and call your name: Isis, Astarte, Diana, Hecate, Demeter, Kali, Inanna! Hear our words. Know our hearts. Be with us in our circle. So mote it be.

- Great Goddess, Lady of the Dark Moon, we thank you for your presence in our circle and in our lives. May you continue to guide and strengthen us in the days to come. So mote it be.

New Moon goddess invocation #2

- Beloved Lady, we call to you to join us tonight as we meet in sacred space. We gather in your name and ask you to help us in our Craft. Guide us to work with wisdom and with love. Welcome, and blessed be.

- Beloved Lady, you have shared with us your wisdom and your love. We thank you for these, and all the gifts that you have given us. Stay if you will, go if you must, in perfect love and perfect trust. So mote it be.

Full Moon goddess invocation #1

- Great Goddess, Lady of the Shining Moon and the Shifting Tides, we your children gather here and invoke your name. On this night of power and beauty, we come together in this sacred space to practice our Craft. Shine your light upon our circle, and lend us your strength and grace. Welcome, and blessed be. (You can say "daughters" instead of "children" if your group is all women.)

- Great Goddess, we thank you for being with us in this circle tonight. May your light and love shine down on us always. Farewell, and blessed be.

Full Moon goddess invocation #2

- Great Lady, we have come together on this, the night of the Full Moon, to work our magick in your name. In perfect love and perfect trust, we gather. In perfect love and perfect trust, we call you to join us. So mote it be.

- Great Lady, we thank you for your presence in our circle and in our lives. Stay if you will, go if you must, in perfect love and perfect trust. So mote it be.

Cakes and ale

We pass cakes and ale around the circle after we have completed the main body of the ritual. The food and drink remind us of our bond with the earth and help to ground us back into the material world. And the act of "breaking bread" together as a symbol of togetherness is as old as society itself.

If you want to keep things simple, you can just say, "We thank the gods for this_____" (whatever you are eating or drinking that night), and pass it around the circle. Most Wiccans do a bit more than that, of course. It is customary for the HPS to bless the cakes and the HP to bless the ale (or the other way around), if a group has both. Or one person can say both blessings if, for example, your group only has a HPS.

Cakes and ale blessing #1

- Cakes: I bless these cakes, gift of the earth. May our blessings multiply like the grains in the fields.

- Ale: I bless this [wine/juice], fruit from the vines. May our lives always be as sweet.

Cakes and ale blessing #2

- Cakes: Bless these cakes, the gift of grain. Sustain us 'til we meet again. So mote it be.

- Ale: Bless this ale, which tastes so sweet. Nourish us 'til again we meet. So mote it be.

Cakes and ale blessing #3

- Cakes: Bless these cakes, the gift of grain, from Earth our bodies to sustain. With gratitude we share this treat. May we always have enough to eat.

- Ale: (The blessing below is a traditional blessing done by the HPS and the HP together. I have seen a number of versions of it, of which this is only one example. It can also be done by the HPS and another group member, or just by the HPS alone. The HPS holds the chalice and the HP holds the athame.)

HP:

Let it be known that no man is greater than a woman.

HPS:

Nor woman greater than a man.

HP:

For what one lacks the other can give.

HPS:

As the chalice is to the female.

HP:

So the athame is to the male.

BOTH TOGETHER:

(HP lowers athame into chalice.) And when they are joined, that is magick in truth—for there is no greater magick in the world than love.

A note about chants

I mentioned a few of the most common chants during some of the rituals. The truth is, I can write out the words, but they aren't much good without the "song" part of the chant. There are a few Wicca websites that go over chants in more detail, but your best bet is to try to find a Witch somewhere who knows them. Or you could make up your own. In the meantime, here are a couple to start with—you can always chant them with no particular music:

- "Isis, Astarte, Diana, Hecate, Demeter, Kali, Inanna." (Repeat)
- "She changes everything She touches and everything She touches changes." (There are a lot more words to this, but many people just use these, repeated over and over.)
- "Fire am I, Water am I, Earth and Air and Spirit am I."

@ Notes

a few basic correspondences for spell work

Love

- Day: Friday
- Color: pink or red (for passion and lust)
- Oil/plant: rose, apple, carnation, clove, lavender, lemon
- Stone: amethyst, rose quartz, turquoise, garnet, moonstone, agate
- Element: Earth
- Runes: Fehu, Kenaz, Gifu, Wunjo, Beorc, Ing

[See the Index of Runes on page 242]

Prosperity

- Day: Thursday
- Color: green
- Oil/plant: basil, cinnamon, clove, ginger, patchouli, peppermint, sandalwood, spearmint
- Stone: aventurine, bloodstone, tigerseye, jade, malachite, mother of pearl, turquoise
- Element: Earth
- Runes: Fehu, Daeg, Othel, Gifu, Uraz, Tir

Health/healing

- Day: Sunday or Monday
- Color: blue (healing and peace), black (banish illness), green (healing and growth)
- Oil/Plant: all healing herbs, especially eucalyptus, rosemary, lemon balm, calendula
- Stone: crystal quartz, amethyst, carnelian, garnet, hematite, bloodstone, lapis, sodalite, turquoise
- Element: All (Fire for banishing illness)
- Runes: Uraz, Kenaz, Sigel, Tir, Ing

Protection

- Day: Sunday or Tuesday
- Color: black, blue, white
- Oil/Plant: rosemary, sage, garlic, basil, dill, juniper, bay
- Stone: black onyx, agate, red jasper, amber, crystal quartz, garnet, tigerseye, malachite, carnelian, amethyst, turquoise
- Element: Fire
- Runes: Thurisaz, Eihwaz, Eolh, Kenaz

Intuition/psychic power

- Day: Tuesday
- Color: purple, silver
- Oil/Plant: lavender, chamomile, frankincense, ginger, myrrh, patchouli, rosemary, sage, vervain
- Stone: amber, amethyst, blue lace agate, lapis, moonstone, crystal quartz
- Element: Water
- Runes: Ansuz, Perdhro, Mannaz, Lagaz

appendix a

new moon and full moon dates

	New Moon Dates:						Full Moon Dates:			
2007	**2008**	**2009**	**2010**	**2011**		**2007**	**2008**	**2009**	**2010**	**2011**
Jan. 18	Jan. 8	Jan. 26	Jan. 15	Jan. 4		Jan. 3	Jan. 22	Jan. 10	Jan. 30	Jan. 19
Feb. 17	Feb. 6	Feb. 24	Feb. 13	Feb. 2		Feb. 2	Feb. 20	Feb. 9	Feb. 28	Feb. 18
Mar. 18	Mar. 7	Mar. 26	Mar. 15	Mar. 4		Mar. 3	Mar. 21	Mar. 10	Mar. 29	Mar. 19
April 17	April 5	April 24	April 14	April 3		April 2	April 20	April 9	April 28	April 17
May 16	May 5	May 24	May 13	May 3		May 2	May 19	May 8	May 27	May 17
June 14	June 3	June 22	June 12	June 1		May 31	June 18	June 7	June 26	June 15
July 14	July 2	July 21	July 11	July 1		June 30	July 18	July 7	July 25	July 15
Aug. 12	Aug. 1	Aug. 20	Aug. 9	July 30		July 29	Aug. 16	Aug. 5	Aug. 24	Aug. 13
Sept. 11	Aug. 30	Sept. 18	Sept. 8	Aug. 28		Aug. 28	Sept. 15	Sept. 4	Sept. 23	Sept. 12
Oct. 11	Sept. 29	Oct. 18	Oct. 7	Sept. 27		Sept. 26	Oct. 14	Oct. 4	Oct. 22	Oct. 11
Nov. 9	Oct. 28	Nov. 16	Nov. 5	Oct. 26		Oct. 26	Nov. 13	Nov. 2	Nov. 21	Nov. 10
Dec. 9	Nov. 27	Dec. 16	Dec. 5	Nov. 25		Nov. 24	Dec. 12	Dec. 2	Dec. 21	Dec. 10
	Dec. 27			Dec. 24		Dec. 23		Dec. 31		

☙ Notes

_____   _____
_____   _____
_____   _____
_____   _____
_____   _____
_____   _____
_____   _____
_____   _____
_____   _____
_____   _____
_____   _____
_____   _____
_____   _____
_____   _____
_____   _____
_____   _____
_____   _____

appendix b

study group topics

As I mentioned in chapter 3, different groups meet on different schedules. If your group has chosen to get together only on New Moons, Full Moons, and sabbats (holidays), then Part 2 of this book contains everything you need for a year's worth of practice.

But if you are like my first group and meet every week, then you will need something else to do during those additional sessions. Here are a few suggestions for study topics. The HPS or HP can lead them all, or group members can take turns researching and presenting a topic. The members of your group will want to discuss which of these topics interest them the most, and they may have some of their own to add as well.

These will also be useful when you have finished your first year of practice together and need some ideas of where to go next in your journey as a group.

Ritual design

How-to, quarter calls, and so on. Gather information about what goes into making a ritual. Each group member can try his or her hand at creating a ritual for an Esbat (Full Moon) or a sabbat, or you can assign each person one component (quarter calls, invocations) and create one together.

Ethics

What does "harm none" really mean? When is it okay to do a spell for someone else? What are the "dos and don'ts" of Witchcraft?

Elements and symbols of Witchcraft

Discuss the elements, the tools we use, the Wheel of the Year, and other important aspects of Wicca. One circle member can research gemstones and another can research candle magick, or you can do a session that covers all the correspondences for healing or prosperity magick.

Gods and goddesses

Take turns presenting information about your favorites, or talk about the way the gods have been viewed in various cultures—Celtic, Egyptian, Greek, Native American, and more.

Pagan history

What really happened in Salem? What were the Burning Times? How and why did the Church push Paganism out of power?

Theology

Why do we believe what we believe? What do we agree on, and where do we differ?

Psychic work and divination

Practice using runes, tarot cards, crystals, and scrying mirrors. What works? What doesn't? What can you do to increase your abilities?

Inner work and self-development

Explore various meditation and relaxation techniques. What are some methods of cleansing, balancing, and mental discipline that work for you?

Magick and energy work

Practical explorations of spells, blessings, and other components of magickal work.

☉ Notes

_____   _____
_____   _____
_____   _____
_____   _____
_____   _____
_____   _____
_____   _____
_____   _____
_____   _____
_____   _____
_____   _____
_____   _____
_____   _____
_____   _____
_____   _____
_____   _____
_____   _____
_____   _____

suggested further reading

There are many wonderful books on Wicca, Witchcraft, and all things magickal. Below are a few of my favorite authors and titles.

Adler, Margot. *Drawing Down the Moon: Witches, Druids, Goddess-Worshippers, and Other Pagans in America Today*. New York: Penguin, 2006 (revised and updated edition).

Originally published more than a quarter-century ago, this is a classic.

Buckland, Raymond. *Buckland's Complete Book of Witchcraft*. St. Paul, MN: Llewellyn, 2002.

One of the original masters. Starts out very traditional, but still full of pertinent information, even for Eclectic Witches.

Cunningham, Scott. *Wicca: A Guide for the Solitary Practitioner*; *Magical Herbalism*; and *The Complete Book of Incense, Oils & Brews*. St. Paul, MN: Llewellyn, various dates.

And everything else he ever wrote. A great source for the basics of all types of magickal work.

Curott, Phyllis. *Book of Shadows: A Modern Woman's Journey into the Wisdom of Witchcraft and the Magic of the Goddess.* New York: Broadway Books, 1998.

This autobiographical account of a successful lawyer's discovery of her inner Witch will strike a chord with others on the same journey of self-discovery.

Dubats, Sally. *Natural Magick.* New York: Citadel, 2002.

Holland, Eileen. *The Wicca Handbook.* York Beach, ME: Samuel Weiser, 2000.

Easy to read and understand, and full of helpful facts.

Johnson, Cait. *Witch in the Kitchen: Magical Cooking for All Seasons.* Rochester, VT: Destiny Books, 2001.

Morrison, Dorothy. *Everyday Moon Magic.* St. Paul, MN: Llewellyn, 2003.

Bringing moon practice into your everyday life.

Peschel, Lisa. *A Practical Guide to the Runes.* St. Paul, MN: Llewellyn, 1989.

The best and simplest all-around guide to the runes that I have found. I keep buying newer, prettier versions of the book—but I always end up using my tattered paperback copy of this one. A must-have if you use runes.

Starhawk. *The Spiral Dance: A Rebirth of the Ancient Religion of the Great Goddess.* San Francisco: HarperSanFrancisco, 1999.

A must-read for every Witch.

Weinstein, Marion. *Positive Magic: Occult Self-Help.* New York: Earth Magic, 1994.

Inspiring and practical, this book captures the essence of what it means to be a Witch.

Wood, Jamie, and Tara Seefeldt. *The Wicca Cookbook: Recipes, Rituals, and Lore.* Berkeley, CA: Celestial Arts, 2000.

Other good authors include:

Patricia Telesco (modern)

Gerina Dunwich (modern)

Judy Harrow (modern)

Gerald Gardner (traditional—one of the founders of the modern Wicca movement)

Janet and Stewart Farrar (traditional—a husband and wife HPS and HP)

And a (very) few helpful sources for supplies:

There are a number of good sources for Wiccan supplies by catalog or online. Unfortunately, I've discovered that many of these seem to disappear as soon as I find them, so I hesitate to include too long a list in this book.

However, there are a few sources that I have repeatedly ordered from with good results, and these have been in existence long enough that I am comfortable recommending them.

For basic supplies and books:

AzureGreen—www.azuregreen.com

48 Chester Rd., Middlefield, MA 01243 USA

Phone: (800) 326-0804

Isis Books and Gifts—www.isisbooks.com

5701 E. Colfax Ave., Denver, CO 80220 USA

Phone: (800) 808-0867

For other Pagan and Wiccan sources and the locations of groups near you:

www.witchvox.com

index of runes

The Runes are an ancient Northern European system of divination. There are 25 runes, including a blank one. The basic meaning and name of each one are listed below, but are by no means comprehensive. Many good books are available to help you learn to use and interpret the Runes. *Compiled by Jennifer Kemper*

Uruz	Othel	Ansuz	Gifu	Mannaz
⊓	◇	↑	✕	ᛗ
strength, healing, will	inheritance, possessions, help	advice, speech, wisdom	partnership, love, gifts	cooperation, humankind, seek advice
Eolh	Eihwaz	Ing	Nied	Perdro
↡	↗	⊗	✝	⊬
protection, friendship, premonition	defense, delay, obstacle	success, relief, milestones	patience, delay, learning	secrets, surprises, mysteries
Tir	Kenaz	Jera	Wunjo	Fehu
↑	⟨	⟐	ᚹ	ᚠ
male, strength, motivation	hearth, power, opening up	rewards, karma, legalities	well-being, happiness, joy	fulfillment, material gain, money
Raidho	Hagall	Lagaz	Ehwaz	Beorc
ᚱ	ᚺ	⌐	ᛗ	ᛒ
journey, strategy, movement	limitation, delays, disruption	female, intuition, imagination	physical movement, travel	family, birth, new love
Wyrd	Sigel	Isa	Daeg	Thurisaz
	⚡	⎮	ᛞ	▷
fate, trust, unknowable	victory, power, success	cessation, standstill, perfidy, freeze	breakthrough, growth, radical change	luck, awakening, thorn

gLossary

Altar: A place to worship (usually holds various tools that are not removed, such as god and goddess candles, incense, and so on).

Athame: A knife, usually double-sided, used for ritual purposes such as pointing and directing energy. It represents the male.

Banishing: Magick done to reduce or get rid of something.

Beltane: Also spelled Beltaine, the pagan holiday that falls on May first.

Book of Shadows: A Witch's book containing rituals, magickal information, and the like.

Cakes and ale: A part of the ritual during which food and drink (not necessarily literally cake or ale) are passed around the circle. It is used for grounding at the end of a ritual and to demonstrate gratitude for our blessings.

Cauldron: A bowl representing the female. Usually made out of metal, it is often fireproof.

Chalice: A cup used during rituals (especially cakes and ale). Also representing the female, this cup should be used only for magickal work and not everyday drinking.

Chant: A song or series of words that are repeated during a ritual in order to raise energy and/or to praise the gods.

Charge of the Goddess: A poem, found in a number of variations, in praise of the goddess (there is also a lesser used *Charge of the God*). Often read during Full Moon rituals.

Circle: A gathering of Witches, or the place where they gather (once the ritual begins, the circle encloses the participants), and another name for a group of Witches.

Cleansing: The act of purifying or cleaning energy, a space, or the like.

Consecrate: To bless, especially when setting something aside for magickal use.

Correspondences: When an item is used to represent a particular property/intent (a rose quartz stone for love, a green candle for prosperity, and so on).

Coven: A group of Witches, usually a group whose members have formally dedicated themselves together.

Craft, The: Another name for Witchcraft.

Crone: The goddess's representation as old woman. Also: a Witch who is an elder.

Dedication: The act of making a formal commitment to the gods. (Witches can be self-dedicated or dedicated by a High Priest and/or High Priestess.)

Deity: A general term for any god or goddess.

Deosil: Movement that is done in a clockwise fashion (usually for increase or positive work).

Element: There are five elements used in Wicca: Earth, Air, Fire, Water, and Spirit.

Esbat: The ritual celebrations that take place at the Full Moon and New Moon.

Garb: Ritual clothing.

Grove: A Druid group.

Handfasting: A pagan wedding ceremony.

High Priest: A male pagan leader.

High Priestess: A female pagan leader.

Hiving off: The term for a new group that is started using at least some members from a preexisting group.

Imbolc: The pagan holiday that falls on February second, and is the origin of Groundhog Day.

Invocation: Words used to summon quarters or invite in a god or goddess.

Intent: The purpose of a spell or magickal working; focused energy.

Lammas/Lughnasadh: The pagan holiday that falls on August first, it is the first of three harvest festivals.

Law of Three: The generally accepted pagan belief that anything put out into the universe will come back threefold.

Litha: Another name for the pagan holiday that falls at Midsummer, or Summer Solstice.

Mabon: The pagan holiday that falls on the Autumn Equinox.

Maiden: The goddess's representation as a young woman.

Mother: The goddess's representation as a nurturing mother.

Mundane: A non-pagan, or everyday life (e.g.: "In my mundane life, I am a librarian").

Old gods: A term for the pagan gods worshipped in earlier times and still worshipped today.

Ostara: The pagan holiday that falls at the Spring Equinox and the origin of the Christian holiday of Easter.

Pagan: A general term for someone who worships the old gods (usually including a goddess figure) and follows a nature-based religion.

Pentacle: A commonly used pagan symbol consisting of a five-pointed star inside a circle. It represents the five elements and the circle of the universe or unity.

Quarter: A direction used in a magickal circle: North, East, South, or West. Each quarter represents specific elements and qualities (North is Earth and grounding, for example.)

Sabbat: Pagan holidays. There are eight sabbats in the pagan year.

Samhain: The pagan holiday that falls on October thirty-first, also known as the Witch's New Year. Samhain is the origin of Halloween.

Smudge stick: An herbal wand used for smudging or cleansing, usually made of sage.

Solitary: A Witch who practices alone.

Speaking stick: A stick or other object that is passed around the circle during ritual. Only the person holding the speaking stick should be talking during this time.

Wheel of the Year: The pagan calendar of holidays. Also: another way of referring to an entire year.

Wicca: A name for one general form of pagan religious practice. All Wiccans are Pagans, but not all Pagans are Wiccans.

Wiccan: One who practices Wicca, also known as a Witch.

Wiccan Rede: The basic rule of Wicca: "An it harm none, do as ye will."

Widdershins: Movement that is done in a counterclockwise direction, usually for unbinding or banishing.

Yule: The pagan holiday that falls on the Winter Solstice and the origin of the Christian holiday of Christmas.

index of magickal work

index

About the author

Deborah Blake, a Wiccan High Priestess, leads her own group, Blue Moon Circle. Prior to founding Blue Moon, she practiced Withcraft for over six years with an Eclectic Witches' study group/circle, and pursued an extensive routine of individual study and spellwork.

When not practicing magick, Deborah makes gemstone jewelry and manages the Artisans' Guild, a not-for-profit artists' cooperative shop that she and a friend founded in 1999.

She lives in rural Upstate New York in a hundred-year-old farmhouse with a Witch's circle behind the barn and the requisite five cats to supervise her activities, pagan and otherwise.

Please visit her website at www.bluemooncircle.net, or e-mail her at magicmysticminerva@ yahoo.com.